Information Technology for Schools

Bena Kallick and James M. Wilson III,
Editors

Sponsored by

The International Network of Principals' Centers

Information Technology for Schools

Creating Practical Knowledge to Improve Student Performance

JOSSEY-BASS
A Wiley Company
San Francisco

Jossey-Bass books and products are available through most bookstores. To contact Jossey-Bass directly, call (888) 378-2537, fax to (800) 605-2665, or visit our website at www.josseybass.com.

Substantial discounts on bulk quantities of Jossey-Bass books are available to corporations, professional associations, and other organizations. For details and discount information, contact the special sales department at Jossey-Bass.

 Manufactured in the United States of America on Lyons Falls Turin Book. This paper is acid-free and 100 percent totally chlorine-free.

Library of Congress Cataloging-in-Publication Data

Information technology for schools : creating practical knowledge to improve student performance / Bena Kallick and James M. Wilson III, editors.— 1st ed.
    p. cm. — (The Jossey-Bass education series)
Includes bibliographical references and index.
ISBN 0-7879-5522-1 (alk. paper)
    1. Computer managed instruction—United States. 2. Academic achievement—United States. 3. Information technology—United States. I. Kallick, Bena. II. Wilson, James M., 1953- III. Series.
LB1028.46 .I533 2000
371.33'4—dc21

                                           00-009568

FIRST EDITION
PB Printing   10 9 8 7 6 5 4 3 2 1

The Jossey-Bass Education Series

Contents

Preface

As they enter the twenty-first century, schools are attempting to implement a systems view of continuous growth and improvement grounded in the careful analysis of data and information. We are now looking at student performance as a way of analyzing what we teach and how we teach it, rather than revisiting our curriculum and instruction as though they were detached from students' responses to them.

Although educators have always been concerned with student performance, they have either allowed measurements to be so poorly aligned with curriculum and instruction that they consider the results untrustworthy or they have paid more attention to programs than they have to the programs' effect on students. Educators tend to have many conversations about special services, for example, but they have few conversations based on their documentation of what works when they are providing those services. They have used research as an add-on to their practices rather than realizing that they, in schools, are also responsible for research that can inform practices so as to improve student performance. They have been willing to be passive to the work of "experts" without realizing what they already know within our schools.

This situation is changing, however. The advent of information technology offers many opportunities and challenges that will change our knowledge of student performance and our practice as educators. This book discusses a number of issues facing educators who are attempting to implement the change to "knowledge work." The issues aggregate around three areas that need attention if schools are to implement information technology and information management successfully and develop knowledge they can use to improve student performance:

- Establishing a solid technological infrastructure
- Using data to create a learning organization through knowledge creation and knowledge management
- Developing the appropriate human resources and ongoing staff development to maintain a learning organization and develop teachers as "knowledge workers"

How a knowledge base and information system can be created to serve a school in order to enhance student performance is still in the formative stages. Many experiments are in progress and effective practices are only beginning to be recognized. The notion of establishing a *knowledge base* is to create an organizational memory of best practices and a means of gathering, sharing, and refining organizational expertise about resources and capabilities that have been observed to be most effective in improving student performance. In a sense, focusing on this organizational knowledge and on the sharing and refining of that knowledge among the practitioners of education is essential to further promote teaching as a truly professional activity. It is through such a community of knowledge that innovations can be shared and the evolution of best practices can be fostered. Information technology provides a medium in which to store, share, and retrieve data and information as never before, and therefore offers the possibility of using that data and information to understand the causes and effects of student performance in our schools.

This book chronicles practitioners' struggles in implementing information technology, identifies the existing barriers to implementation, and provides a set of frameworks from our current understanding of this process to support learning through knowledge creation. The various chapters ask a fundamental question: *Can technology help build a learning organization that is driven by data, infor-*

mation, and knowledge gathered on curriculum, instruction, and assessment so as to inform decisions about student learning and programs?

The initial chapter in the book describes a process that facilitates knowledge creation: the feedback spiral (Costa and Kallick, 1994). This model delineates a rational process of planning, implementation, and data collection and assessment to guide any process within an organization. This process is presented at the outset as an integrating idea that is revisited in subsequent chapters. The purpose is to reinforce knowledge creation as an ongoing process that does indeed have a method.

The book then turns to accounts from practitioners who are attempting to implement technology and information systems. Superintendents Ben Norman in Ankeny, Iowa, and Sherry P. King in Mamaroneck, New York, both manage districts that have exerted considerable effort to develop their technological infrastructure. Given this push to "lay down the train tracks," these authors revisit the question of where they are going. The question they are now facing is how to make use of the hardware and software they have in terms of knowledge creation in order to better manage the organization. As is often the case in the evolution of information systems, the vision for hardware is initially developed beyond the capacity of the organization to make use of what is available. In Chapter Two, Norman discusses the political process of establishing these technological resources and shares his vision of the future use of technology for improving student performance. In Chapter Three, King critiques the existing information infrastructure and shares her vision of creating a learning organization based on accessible and timely information that can answer the question, How are our kids doing?

The management of a successful information system is complex. It requires both vision and the daily capacity to attend to details. To help integrate the components of technology, knowledge creation, and human resource development, Jonathan P. Costa Sr. and Esther Bobowick, consultants in Connecticut, provide in Chapter Four an approach to organizational assessment that considers each of these components. These authors show how an organization can begin to collect data so as to start the process of knowledge creation that can yield an answer to the question, *Does technology matter in terms of student performance?* Developing a process for collecting these data will create information that will reveal trends and eventually, when linked to policy interventions and other variables, yield knowledge. These authors give us a solid first step on the long journey of knowledge creation.

In Chapter Five, we move into the classroom. How do teachers observe technology making a difference in the classroom? Authors Kenneth C. Holvig and Gerald Crisci are teachers at Scarsdale, New York, public schools who work with classroom teachers to provide technological assistance. They see their role as coaches for teachers as well as students. Their work raises important concerns about who is leading whom in the process of learning about technology and knowledge creation. These authors provide a framework for delivering technology-enhanced instruction and tell us what to look for in the classroom to observe the effects of such instruction. They also present their views on what is needed to sustain technology-enhanced instruction in schools.

In Chapter Six, Barbara Schain Spitz and Madge Hildebrandt Klais outline how action research can be used in schools to develop knowledge. This brief chapter sets the stage for the action research described by Hildebrandt Klais in Chapter Seven.

How has technology changed learning, or individual knowledge creation? The broad range of information now available to students through the Internet has caused Hildebrandt Klais, a librarian from Sherman Middle School in Madison, Wisconsin, to be concerned with the importance of research skills in guiding students in an environment saturated with information. In Chapter Seven, she develops a framework for examining the use of information technology via the methodology of action research, a strategy for practitioners to engage in research as a way to build knowledge in the organization. She provides an extensive analysis of student research and offers tools for interested readers to replicate her process.

A critical concern in implementing information technology is human resource development. In Chapter Eight, Esther Bobowick, a staff developer from Connecticut, discusses her work with an elementary school in Fairfield, Connecticut, where a group of teachers and administrators approach the question of how to enhance the human resources of their school to better support the use of technology and knowledge creation. The author presents and discusses the unique conditions that information technology poses for human resource development.

The final, integrating chapter by Bena Kallick and James M. Wilson III provides an overview of critical issues that an organization must face to implement a knowledge-creating organization successfully. We delineate a set of challenges faced by organizations in attempting to implement information technology and the process of the feedback spiral to support knowledge creation. In this chapter, we integrate the observations of the previous chapters to provide a systems view of knowledge creation via information technology in schools. The aim is to leave the reader with some solid tools for sense-making about information technology and knowledge creation with the goal of improving student performance.

August 2000   Bena Kallick
Guilford, Connecticut
James M. Wilson III
Amherst, Massachusetts

Reference

Costa, A., and Kallick, B. *Assessment in the Learning Organization*. Alexandria, Va.: Association for Supervision and Curriculum Development, 1994.

The International Network of Principals' Centers

The International Network of Principals' Centers sponsors periodicals and other publications as part of its commitment to strengthening leadership at the individual school level through professional development for leaders. Back issues of *New Directions for School Leadership*, formerly published as a quarterly journal, are now available and upcoming publications will be available from Jossey-Bass. The network has a membership of principals' centers, academics, and practitioners in the United States and overseas and is open to all groups and institutions committed to the growth of school leaders and the improvement of schools. It currently functions primarily as an information exchange and support system for member centers in their efforts to work directly with school leaders in their communities. The network's office is in the Principals' Center at the Harvard Graduate School of Education.

The Network offers the following services:

- The International Directory of Principals' Centers features member centers, listing contact persons, center activities, program references, and evaluation instruments.
- The Annual Conversation takes place every spring; members meet for seminars and workshops, to listen to speakers, and to initiate discussions that will continue throughout the year.
- *Newsnotes*, the network's quarterly newsletter, informs members about programs, conferences, workshops, and special-interest items.

- *Reflections*, the annual journal, includes articles by principals, staff developers, university educators, and principals' center staff members.

For further information, please contact:

International Network of Principals' Centers
Harvard Graduate School of Education
8 Story Street, Lower Level
Cambridge, MA 02138
(617) 495–9812
(617) 495–5900 (Fax)
inpce@gse.harvard.edu

The Editors

Bena Kallick is a private consultant providing services to school districts, state departments of education, professional organizations, and public agencies throughout the United States and abroad. Kallick received her doctorate in educational evaluation at Union Graduate School. Her areas of focus include group dynamics, creative and critical thinking, and alternative assessment strategies for the classroom. Her written work includes *Literature to Think About* (a whole language curriculum published by Weston Woods Studios, 1985), *Changing Schools into Communities for Thinking* (originally published by North Dakota Study Group on Research and Evaluation, 1989; published in 1998 by Technology Pathways, Guilford, Connecticut), *Assessment in the Learning Organization*, coauthored with Arthur Costa (Association for Supervision and Curriculum Development, 1995), and *Habits of Mind* (a four-book series published by the Association for Supervision and Curriculum Development, 2000), coauthored with Arthur Costa.

Formerly a Teachers' Center director, Kallick also created a children's museum based on problem solving and invention. She was the coordinator of a high school alternative designed for at-risk students. She is cofounder of Technology Pathways Corporation, a company dedicated to providing easy-to-use software that helps integrate and make sense of data from curriculum, instruction, and assessment. Kallick's teaching appointments have included Yale University School of Organization and Management, University of Massachusetts Center for Creative and Critical

Thinking, and Union Graduate School. She was formerly on the board of the Apple Foundation and is presently on the board of Jobs for the Future.

James M. Wilson III is cofounder, along with Bena Kallick, of Technology Pathways Corporation, where he focuses on knowledge engineering in schools to help teachers develop useful information on student performance. Wilson is also founder and director of Data and Decision Analysis, a management consulting firm that develops decision support systems for organizations. Over the past fifteen years he has worked with sixteen state educational agencies, as well as numerous school districts, to improve their use of information. Wilson has an M.B.A., an M.S. in applied economics, and a Ph.D. in strategic management. He has written numerous articles on the use of information to guide strategic decision making in organizations, and he specializes in the use of computer simulation to model and test theories of organizational and market processes. He has authored more than twenty pieces of software.

The Contributors

Esther Bobowick is an education consultant in Sandy Hook, Connecticut.

Jonathan P. Costa Sr. is an education consultant in Litchfield, Connecticut.

Gerald Crisci is director of instructional computing in the Scarsdale Public Schools, Scarsdale, New York.

Kenneth C. Holvig is head computer teacher at Scarsdale Middle School, Scarsdale, New York.

Sherry P. King is superintendent of the Mamaroneck Public Schools, Mamaroneck, New York.

Madge Hildebrandt Klais is coordinator of Library Media Services, Madison Metropolitan School District, Madison, Wisconsin.

Ben Norman is superintendent of the Ankeny Community School District, Ankeny, Iowa.

Barbara Schain Spitz is technology integration specialist for the Madison Metropolitan School District, Madison, Wisconsin.

Chapter One

A Model for Organizational Learning

The Feedback Spiral

Bena Kallick, James M. Wilson III

Creating practical knowledge requires a method of
inquiry over time to guide organizational change.

A new mental model is called for as we harness the power of technology to help our schools continuously improve the education of our children. In the past, we have often thought of assessment as a process of judging, sorting, and categorizing. It has been perceived as a way to discriminate and create groups of exclusion and inclusion. As we move into the twenty-first century, and given the demands of an information-driven society, we recognize the need for a higher level of thinking skills for our entire population. This need has brought us to an examination of our standards and assessments. We are raising questions about how good is good enough, and how can we elicit more from all of our students, realizing that schools must provide the educational foundation for life-long learning.

The knowledge-based workplace requires new skills that focus more specifically on critical thinking, analysis, evaluation, inquiry, and experimentation. In her book *In the Age of the Smart Machine*, Shoshana Zuboff (1988) discusses the impact of technology on the workplace. She refers to a shift away from the workplace as "action centered" to the workplace that requires "intellective" skills. She states that the shift to intellective skills "encompasses a shift away from physical cues, toward sense-making based more exclusively upon abstract cues; explicit inferential reasoning used both inductively and deductively; and procedural, systemic thinking" (p. 95). When we apply that definition to a school environment, it has implications for all members of the learning community. For administrators, it means a greater dedication and support for information gathering and analysis across departments and grade levels. For teachers, it means a greater dedication to the collection of data about student performance that can be shared in a more public way. It means that teachers will have not only to continue to collect information through their senses and impressions, but will also have to collect data systematically that can be compared reliably to the work in other classrooms. Students will have to learn how to construct meaning from multiple data sources. They will need to learn how to work in teams, communicate with one another effectively, and become self-directed in their learning. A significant part of learning for all members of the learning community will be the demonstration of the capacity to become self-evaluative, receive feedback, and be responsive to evaluation, with a drive for higher-quality performances. The organization will be propelled by knowledge workers.

Given that the means to achieve these results from students is still in the formative stage, we need a model to guide the process of developing knowledge about what does and does not work in attempting to meet these challenging goals.

Feedback Spirals

The image of a feedback spiral (Costa and Kallick, 1994) encompasses the concepts of repetition and movement. The steps in the process repeat, but there is new learning all the while that leads to a broader understanding of what is being observed. Tracking how events occur over time and the history of our assumptions is fundamental to this process. This is the importance of *feedback*—the horizontal dimension of this process—revisiting the initiative and analyzing its result. Feedback spirals suggest a model for thinking that is based on the evolutionary nature of knowledge creation. Feedback alone generates a static loop if nothing is learned. The *spiral* suggests the vertical dimension of this process—learning that can alter knowledge and therefore assumptions and policies.

For example, rather than seeing assessment data as a judgment, the feedback spiral suggests that we see the data as an opportunity to build knowledge. Each score in a given test is considered data. A collection of scores show emerging patterns that provide us with information about the direction our policies are taking to improve student performance. When we understand the cause of the patterns, we are constructing knowledge. This knowledge of cause and effect provides us with some measure of prediction, and it leads us to new hypotheses about the work we are doing. This may lead us to modify our policies. If we do, we then scrutinize the results in a subsequent period. This process of adaptive learning is illustrated in Figure 1.1.

The feedback spiral has six iterative steps.

1. We start by determining our purposes and goals and *setting benchmarks* (1A). What are we trying to do? Why are we focused on this aspect of our work? What do we hope the outcome of our work will be? We set benchmarks and indicators for what success will look like if we do the work well.

2. Now we need to *plan* (2A). What process or approach will we adopt to the proposed work? Who needs to be involved? What is our time line? What are the actions we plan to take and when?

3. When we *implement* (3A), we are taking the plan to action. The actions we take are our opportunity for learning, as the results are often not what was expected or intended.

4. However, learning will only take place if we collect information about the results. It is in the *assessment* (4A) phase that we gather evidence to be studied after the implementation.

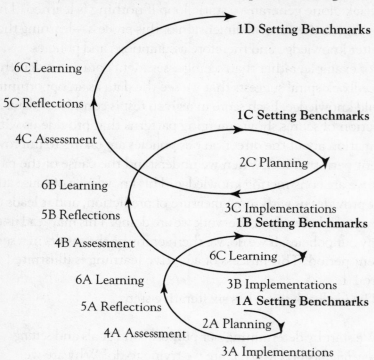

Figure 1.1. The Process of Adaptive Learning.

5. Too often, we are ready to stop at this point and make judgments. Instead, the spiral suggests *analysis and reflection* (5A). This should be done collectively so that multiple perspectives are considered. It is at this point that we seek patterns from the information before us. We raise questions and hypotheses about the causes for the patterns. We make assumptions and learn to challenge our assumptions.

6. Step five creates the basis for *learning* (6A). We make some decisions about how we might modify the changes we have implemented and the assumptions that guide us on the basis of what we have learned, and we enter the next iteration of the spiral.

A thoughtful district is guided by multiple spirals. That is, this process is used by students in their learning, by teachers in analyzing their instructional strategies, and by administrators in analyzing assessments and curriculum.

Example: Using the Feedback Spiral to Focus on Administration

This process has real-time value. For example, reports to boards of education can be guided over time by the use of feedback spirals as a way of observing the effective changes in the district. The board can ask for reports based on this process rather than reports that reduce to numbers.

When the board guides its decisions on the basis of reports from the feedback spiral, a different level of rationality and restraint occurs. Rather than seeing change, at whatever cost, as a positive force, the feedback spiral presses the board to understand the change process and inquire specifically about where the district is in this process. Since the spiral has specific points of activity, the board can have a work session to review each aspect, beginning with the purpose for the innovation or program change. A report can be presented by an English department, for example, that responds to the question of how technology has enhanced student learning. The department chair can organize the report by walking through the spiral:

1. *Purpose:* We initiated the use of technology in our writing labs and provided technical assistance for students so that they could use the computer to write and revise papers. Our goal was to influence the way students think about writing, given the technology available.

2. *Planning:* We decided to focus on the tools in word processing that would be of particular assistance to the writing process. We discovered software that would help the students brainstorm as a prewriting activity. We provided opportunities for students to learn keyboarding skills, if they were not already in place. We made certain that students knew how to multitask, set up a table of contents,

set up footnotes and bibliography, and edit efficiently. We decided to use a combination of the writing lab, the computer lab, and the classroom teacher to implement this program.

3. *Implementation:* We organized our schedules and resources so that all incoming ninth grade students would have an opportunity to learn the necessary skills for producing the required writing across the curriculum in the high school.

4. *Assessment:* We collected samples of student writing on a monthly basis so that we could chart the growth and improvement. We used the state scoring rubric to score these selected papers. In addition, we collected metacognitive reflections from students regarding their shifts in thinking about writing, given the use of technology.

5. *Reflection and evaluation:* The group of teachers involved in the innovation met on a monthly basis to analyze the writing papers and study the results. We reflected on the wisdom of using our resources in this way.

6. *Modifications based on data:* We realized by mid-year that we were able to change the program. All students did not need the additional support and technical assistance. Many had progressed beyond what we were offering. We created a special situation for the students who continued to need extra help. We realized that we needed to have a first-semester use of resources and a second-semester redistribution of resources.

7. *Return to purposes, goals, and outcomes:* We continue to see this focus on technology and writing across the curriculum as valuable. Students entering high school should know how to use technology effectively to help them meet the rigorous writing assignments required in their work. Although many have access to computers at home, we still find it necessary to instruct use of the tools available to enhance the writing process.

If a report were produced as above, the board could interact with each event within the spiral. The board members could see the writing results through the lens of a carefully engineered process. They could question the decisions made by the English department. Most significantly, such a report could serve as a systematic review of a new practice. Since many boards do not receive such reports, they often take a freewheeling stance with the work of schools. Board members tend to use their own child's experiences or the experiences of parents who call them as a guide to their thinking. Systematic reporting can provide a richer database for evaluating the choices the schools are making. However, systematic reporting should include process as well as product.

Example: Using the Feedback Spiral to Focus on Learning

In an elementary school, the problem presented was how to coordinate all the services that were being provided for the increasing number of programs for English as a second language (ESL), special education, speech, reading, and counseling. Using a model from programming, we considered the student the object of these services. To this point, the school collectively had been focused on services rather than the student who was receiving the services. When we placed the student as the object of inquiry, we started asking the following questions: How many of us see the same students? How can we communicate with one another about the student's progress? How do we communicate with the classroom teacher about support for these students in the classroom in a coordinated way?

We began to realize that we could begin to create a system, by using technology, that would help us think this through. We began with our *purposes and goals*: to serve as many students as thoughtfully as possible. We discussed the outcomes we felt we needed to benchmark to make certain that students were prepared for a high-stakes state test.

We moved on to *planning* for learning for the students. We realized that we had little documented information about what works for the student as an intervention. For example, the speech teacher could identify what she thought worked for a student, but she did not have documented evidence. And since she was under extreme pressure to see as many students as possible, she was unable to think through what was worthy of documentation. Using the feedback spiral as a mental map, we thought about a plan for the students who were being served. We designed a "swat team" of teachers who would assess all students in the first grade.

To *implement* this, each member of the team—consisting of the classroom teacher, the psychologist, the resource teacher, the special education teacher, the speech teacher, the reading teacher, the principal, and assistant principal—would be responsible for testing five to six students in the first grade. The assessments would be designed from already existing methodologies within the building, such as a letter and word recognition inventory. We established a small battery of tests and designed a plan for how testing would take place in the fall.

After the diagnostic was performed, student referrals were determined. Each referral was entered in a database and a student record was initiated. As instruction proceeded, student progress was documented, as well as the instruction that caused the progress. After a few months, another diagnostic effort was made. At this point we could engage in *assessment*—we were able to compare the data from the first testing with the data from the January testing. Since we had documented instruction and student progress, we were also able to identify what sort of instructional strategies were most powerfully employed to the benefit of the student.

As we *reflected* on the test results and other information, we realized that we had far more explicit knowledge about what works with what sorts of problems. This provided a rich opportunity for the classroom teachers (who participated in the analysis of results) to learn new strategies and *modify* what they might use with these students in the classroom.

Our conversation began in April with a group of frustrated, stressed, special education teachers who were feeling that the classroom teachers did not know enough about these students to implement practices that would reinforce their learning and growth. By the end of January, there was a sense of team—a feeling of the collective wisdom of the group, including the classroom teachers. The feedback spiral had provided a rich cycle of learning and a recognizable process on how to engage in rational organizational change. Considerable learning had taken place about the students and about how to implement the plan differently next time.

Conclusion

If an organization is to be a learning organization it must engage in critical self-inquiry at all levels. Given the imperatives of the post-industrial, post-modern, information age, a process for engaging in rational communicative inquiry is essential. Technology is driving this imperative and can promote its successful outcome. The much greater capability to share, store, present, and retrieve information presents us with the challenge of organizing a workflow and process of continuous improvement that can harness this data processing power to create knowledge to improve student performance.

To do this at the organizational level requires coordination of technological resources, development of a shared information system, and cultivation of human resources so that educators can become knowledge workers. That is our challenge as advocates of education. The feedback spiral can play an important role in conquering this challenge by preventing us from simply going around in circles.

References

Costa, A., and Kallick, B. *Assessment in the Learning Organization*. Alexandria, Va.: Association for Supervision and Curriculum Development, 1994.
Zuboff, S. *In the Age of the Smart Machine*. New York: Basic Books, 1988.

Chapter Two

Involving Stakeholders in Developing Technology

Ben Norman

> Creating a learning community means staying
> focused on gathering the resources to make it
> happen and staying in touch with the large
> community of education stakeholders.

In public institutions it is common to hear that it takes three to five years to initiate a program or process. If that is the case, tenure of leadership becomes an issue. For example, if it takes two to three years to become established as a superintendent, and three to five years to institutionalize a program, tenures of less than six to eight years probably will not make substantial changes in the system. If we take seriously the work that the district must do to be a part of the community, we realize that long-term leadership plus community involvement will build the learning community we seek. I have been the Ankeny Community School District's superintendent for twenty-three years. Over the years I have noticed that when people work together, they tend to support what they create. And if the group working together represents various viewpoints on the issue, the outcome is generally supported by the community.

The Beginning

Every story needs to have a beginning. Ours began twelve years ago with the planning of a new building. We knew technology was going to be a major player in our future and we wanted to make certain that this new building would be a pivotal example for our district.

The district developed a collaborative decision-making model to address change and seek involvement of the staff. This model established a decision-making process that gradually became an opportunity for staff to be involved with decisions that affect them directly, with the realization that staff have little interest in playing the middle manager or central manager's role. At the same time, we built a collaborative process with the community. The city and district work closely together on many issues. These collaborations started with simple issues and progressed over the years. We now share resources. Our print shop procures items for the city, and the city parks and recreation department uses the district facilities without cost for their programs. The city uses district buses and works together on playground projects. The city provides the district with large equipment for snow removal and asphalt patching and provides sand and salt. These examples are a clear demonstration of the collaborative arrangements that have saved each of us significant dollars in duplication.

Building the Infrastructure

With collaboration as a theme, the development of our new building was launched. Both staff and community were involved in our pursuit of an excellent infrastructure for technology. We took staff and administrators to educational and business sites that were using technology effectively. We observed firsthand the skills students would need to be technologically literate in their work after graduating from our high school. We sent teachers, maintenance staff, administrators, and board members to conferences and workshops. Local businesses allowed us to participate in their training programs. In addition, the National School Board Association Institute for the Transfer of Technology to Education was extremely helpful.

With the need for technology clearly established, we developed a funding strategy. We knew that people need to have technology available to use as they are trained, and the infrastructure needs to be in place and working for people to be willing and able to use this resource. It is indeed the case: "If you build it, they will come." So our first order of business was building the infrastructure.

The consultants we found most helpful were those who were able actively to engage our staff. We thought about how people would use the technology: by the time we answered the consultant's questions, we had a good sense of what we wanted. Consultants and technicians proved to be important for the engineering side of the decisions. Second opinions are nice, but there are many right ways to build a complicated technology system. We developed the goal of keeping our support systems two years ahead to make certain the technology is ready to work when the staff is ready for it.

We did not hire a technology director because we felt that there would never be enough people to support the questions that would come up. Instead, we built a strong staff development program and secured our media staff to be the first in line. It is only now, twelve years later, that we are considering hiring a technology coordinator to work districtwide in further facilitating our use of technology and hiring work-process technicians to manage our system. We have used our in-house "techies" to help teachers, and students are a significant part of our support for classroom use of technology.

Knowledge Management and Creation

In accordance with Iowa state requirements, at the same time that we were building the system, we were also developing "District Essential Learnings," district standards and benchmarks and district assessments. That work created an impetus for using technology to manage the many curriculum and assessment documents that were developed. We came face to face with a most significant shift in the culture. For the first six years of development, technology infrastructure drove our decisions. In the past few years, curriculum, instruction, and assessment have driven our decisions. We are now seeking: individual student records and ways to link those records to our curriculum maps, mapping our assessments and linking the data we collect from multiple forms of assessment, and communicating with parents and our community from Web sites and Web pages.

We are exploring electronic portfolios as a way to bring the student voice into the assessment work that we do. We have invited a group of teachers to work on developing portfolios that are constructed by students. This activity brought twenty teachers voluntarily to the conversation about what technology really can offer portfolios. The teachers have discovered the need for a multimedia portfolio, one that will include print as well as video and audio as appropriate forms. The combined result will be the pilot work for next year.

In each of the above examples we are learning that the infrastructure is only a small part of our quest for excellence. We must also understand when technology is the best medium and when it is not. We have decided to expose students to a variety of software and hardware, including both Macintosh and PC. We know that the world beyond school requires a great deal of flexibility and tolerance for change. A single-system response, with only high-end equipment, may not be sufficient experience for entering this world.

Developing Our Human Resources

We had staff development for use of technology from day one. However, six years ago, as our hardware and equipment purchases were to a point that everyone could easily get access to the systems, we asked staff what they felt should be the expectations for teacher competency. Staff were asked to develop a set of competencies collaboratively. They identified the competencies, designed a program (for which the media staff served as the monitors), and set about teaching themselves or getting outside help for their learning. One attempt was to have a special staff development offering in August for a week. This proved to be very successful. Staff are also in the process of developing a computer experience outside the curriculum for students in grades six through twelve with high interest in technology. Teachers and students often join learning in after-school programs offered in the computer lab.

Conclusion

The learning community concept pushes the district and community to seek additional ways to incorporate the community into the district's plans. We are presently working to connect the city library with the school's library system. The library and the middle school facility has also been considered as a possible location for a joint school-community satellite site. The idea of a communitywide network is also being discussed. To support these resources, the district is working on connecting our facilities via fiber optic cable to allow the resources at every site to be shared with all sites. We feel that fiber cable will reduce our operational costs.

The learning community includes school staff in collaboration with the broader community in which the schools reside. As the school district grows in student population, there is a lack of resources to address that growth. This has fostered many collaborations that probably have better outcomes than if we had done the work separately. Each success has led to further consideration: *What comes next?* With the community and the district working together, each accomplished goal establishes a new goal.

Chapter Three

Tracking Data on Student Achievement

Questions and Lessons

Sherry P. King

> Developing an information system to answer
> questions about student performance means taking
> a close look at current practices with a vision of
> what is possible.

How are our kids doing? The answer depends on who is asking the question. Sometimes, the answer calls for specific information about a child's progress in relation to what a child of that age might be expected to know and be able to do; for example, whether or not a child is reading on grade level. At other times, the focus is more generic: At what colleges were high school seniors accepted? Ask a teacher how her kids are doing and in addition to content knowledge, she may share observations about students' ability to cooperate, work independently, self-correct, and become deeply engaged in learning. For administrators, answering the question often means finding the balance between the progress of individual students and the achievements of all of the students in the school or district. Board members, looking for longitudinal information about student achievement to assess the health of the system, try to balance the stories of individual children and parents against the achievements of the district as a whole.

Regardless of who is asking how our kids are doing, answering the questions means gathering data, thinking about what the data show and don't show, and using that information to help make decisions about the future. Given our district's immersion in technology, I imagined that with a click of a button I could get information on any question about student achievement. Instead, I find myself in a constant scavenger hunt: sifting through mountains of data that exist throughout the system but are rarely available in a form that can help answer questions about what we can do to help improve our students' achievement.

The Scavenger Hunt

An offhand comment by one parent about the number of students who were in accelerated math in eighth grade led me to wonder about how many students who had achieved mastery on the state's sixth grade math test made it to the highest level of math our middle school offered. Because admission into the accelerated math course is crucial to students' having the opportunity to take the highest level of math in the high school, the district is committed to supporting as many middle school students as are able in accelerated math. Trying to use our information system to assess our students' progress in math and improve our program has been a challenging project.

At the same time that I began to investigate the pattern of math placement in our middle school, high school test results for nonaccelerated students raised concerns about their ability to succeed. We decided to analyze the tests to determine what we had to do to help all our students improve their achievement. As we met with secondary math teachers, they speculated that many of the students who were in danger of not graduating because of failing a math competency test had come to this school as older students who were "illiterate" in their native language. Did I have information that could confirm or refute this claim? For these and countless other concerns, each question led me on a new hunt for information.

To find out about the students in accelerated math I had to pursue several data sources: the current roster of students (middle school database), sixth grade scores on state exams (cumulative folders in the middle school guidance office), designation of mastery for eighth-graders on their sixth grade tests (testing and assessment database, which is located in the high school), and analysis of the scores against the current class lists. That work, which required several weeks of effort, suggested some interesting findings.

The initial insight was technological in nature: We lack an integrated database that could help us answer questions such as who has access to accelerated courses. The next findings shed new light on our educational program. First, a significant proportion of students who achieved mastery in sixth grade, and received very high grades in seventh grade, were not in accelerated math in eighth grade. Second, a disproportionately high number of students who fit that profile also came from our most economically diverse elementary school. This information suggested several possibilities. Did all our elementary schools send students to the middle school with the same foundation of math knowledge and skills? Was the instructional program at the middle school designed to enable all students to have access to the accelerated program? Did students in all levels of math at the middle school share the same curriculum? Was there real or perceived bias against students from a particular elementary school? This "hidden" information had significant implications for everyone in the system. It called for an evaluation of the math program at the elementary schools. It required an evaluation of how students were placed at the middle school. It necessitated a review of all curriculum for all students to determine whether they were all receiving the opportunities to learn that would allow them to excel.

The casual remark by a parent opened the door to review of our math program and the realization that otherwise helpful data were too scattered to be immediately useful. The process of answering questions about math crystallized my frustration with an information system that was not designed to help. These examples highlight the challenges of living in a system that has an enormous amount of data but still functions as though it is information-poor. At the systems level, the amount of effort involved in each of these scavenger hunts was far too labor-intensive to be an effective way to make systemwide decisions. However, we need data to understand whether the way in which we allocate resources supports enhanced student achievement. Our schools are not unlike most schools in implementing programs and continuing to fund them without evidence of their success. In a time of limited resources, we need a way to build in accountability, not for the purpose of sanctions, but to enable the system to change according to what best supports students' learning. For example, our high school had offered a regents-level science course (a rigorous New York State regents exam is required to pass such a course) over a year and a half for students who were struggling in science. Although everyone cheered this effort to raise expectations for students, actual student results suggested that their academic success was not significantly better for having been in the extended class.

Looking at the data forced us to find another way to provide support for those students to achieve. Similarly, we have scheduled extra "lab" periods for students who are struggling with the college-level math curriculum in the high school. From the beginning, we decided that we would try this new approach for two years and analyze the student achievement data to determine whether we would continue with this model.

The question is not whether we will support struggling students, but how we can gather our data that will show us whether present programming supports struggling students. The only way we can know that is by harnessing the information to provide evidence that can help us make decisions about whether initiatives are truly helping improve student learning. How to harness the information becomes the greatest question of all.

From Student Records to Student Profiles

In the winter of 1998 we decided to use the opportunity of our K–12 math initiative that grew out of the scavenger hunt just described to see whether we could build an integrated information system that would help us systematically gather and analyze assessment data. As with much of technology, the hard work has been in the discussions and decisions about what is important, not in the technology itself. Jim Wilson, a consultant from Technology Pathways, began a process to move our district toward the kind of information system that would help us gather longitudinal information on student achievement that we could use for continuous improvement. As superintendent, I want to know (1) whether our new math curriculum helps all students achieve to their maximum potential in keeping with New York State's standards; (2) whether we are targeting resources to ensure appropriate opportunities for all students to learn; (3) whether, given appropriate supports, our minority and economically disadvantaged students are achieving at levels similar to their peers. In order to address these questions, we brought together principals, guidance counselors, math teachers, and data gathering and analysis experts.

Despite his background in technology and information systems, Jim Wilson's entree into our school system had nothing to do with computers. Rather, he began with confidential, in-depth conversations about what data each person wanted, used, or thought the system had. After extensive interviews and follow-up surveys, Jim produced a graphic representation of the data our system has on student achievement (see Table 3.1).

This visual image was striking in its presentation. First, it made clear that all the information in the system appears in discrete, disconnected records. Second, there was virtually no link between data sources. For example, the information in the elementary cumulative record folders was not linked to the state standards, standardized tests, or the state exams, nor was it available through computers. Third, the data in the system did not add up to a comprehensive profile of student achievement. Although we believe that student achievement is multifaceted, the graphic representation of the data in the system showed a one-dimensional student record. Neither data nor technological ability alone would be enough to create a rich profile of student achievement. Rather, Jim's inquiry demonstrated that as a system we had to make decisions about what data

Table 3.1. Preliminary Inventory of Mamaroneck Data on Students: Focus on Math.

Grade	Stanford Achievement	PEP (Phased Out)	Differential Aptitude Test (DAT)	SAT	Regents Exams	Local Exams (Mid Term, Final)	District Criterion Reference Test	Final Grades (4/Year)	Parent Conference Form	NYS Math Assessment Pilot	Teacher Anecdotal
Pre-K											
K									Cum. Folder		
1									Cum. Folder		
2									Cum. Folder		
3	Cum. Folder	Cum. Folder							Cum. Folder		
4	Cum. Folder						Cum. Folder		Cum. Folder	Cum. Folder	
5	Cum. Folder										

Grade				
6	📁 Cum. Folder	📇 Access & Mini	📇 Mini	📁 Cum. Folder
7	📁 Cum. Folder	📇 Access & Mini	📇 Mini	📁 Cum. Folder
8	📁 Cum. Folder	📇 Access & Mini	📇 Mini	📁 Cum. Folder & Placement Rec.
9	📇 Access & Mini	📁 Cum. Folder	📇 Mini	📇 Mini
10	PSAT 📁 Cum. Folder	📇 Access & Mini	📁 Cum. Folder	📇 Mini
11	SAT I 📇 Mini	📇 Access & Mini	📁 Cum. Folder	📇 Mini

(Continued)

Table 3.1. Continued.

Grade	Stanford Achievement	PEP (Phased Out)	Differential Aptitude Test (DAT)	SAT	Regents Exams	Local Exams (Mid Term, Final)	District Criterion Reference Test	Final Grades (4/Year)	Parent Conference Form	NYS Math Assessment Pilot	Teacher Anecdotal
12				SAT II ⌂ Cum. Folder	▭ Access & Mini	⌂ Cum. Folder		▭ Mini			

Key: ⌂ = Hard copy, not on electronic media

▭ = On electronic media ("Mini" = Minicomputer, "Access" = indicates data are stored on a microcomputer in Microsoft Access) we would gather that would show students' work in a number of domains. Then we could use our technology to share the information for use in student placement, curricular decisions, or staff development. We are now building such a system with Jim. With an information system that provides data on content knowledge as well as performance ability, we can provide meaningful accountability to parents and policymakers and gain insights into how students will best benefit from the use of our resources.

We are continuing our work with Jim, coordinating the integration of an information management system that will allow us access to all our existing sources of information that is relevant to student performance in mathematics. Simultaneously, we have been exploring the question of what the math scavenger hunt suggests at the school and classroom level. Again, our work in math serves as a model for any discipline.

Assessment, Classroom Practice, and Systemic Reform

Our math case studies show that our schools are typical: they are filled with information that is often ignored in practice. Moving to a data-driven system with high accountability represents a shift in culture. To help prepare for this change in Mamaroneck, the board of education allowed the schools a two-year window to pilot a host of new assessments without reporting the results to parents or the board itself. The purpose was to provide a window of opportunity for the staff to take a hard look at their strengths and weaknesses and have time to improve practice before moving into a time of public accountability for the new assessments.

During the pilot period, the central office staff and building administrators initiated a new way of combining attention to assessment with some of the potential of technology. We decided to disaggregate achievement data by individual classroom, provide an item analysis for each class assessment, and share that information with the teachers. Principals received computer-generated information that gave them information about individual students, classrooms, and grade levels. Rather than employing the usual model of giving a standardized test at the end of the year and basically ignoring the results because the students had already moved on, we worked to help all the teachers understand what the results suggested about their instructional practice and how their students achieved relative to other students in the school and across the district. In some cases, it was clear that some classes had not covered certain material.

In other cases, there were specific concepts that students generally did not understand. In yet other classes, students were ignoring some basic skills even as they were mastering more sophisticated material. Across the district, there were clear examples of best practices that teachers could share with each other. In all cases, this level of detailed information was new to teachers. There were some uncomfortable conversations as people began to relate the results of their individual classes. There were also helpful sharing sessions as teachers began to describe successful strategies for teaching. The entire initiative helped in the district's effort to break the isolation of classroom practice and create opportunities for teachers to support each other and all students in reaching the goals that were not yet public but soon would be.

During this pilot process, a group of teachers from across the district began to work with *Techpaths for Math*. *Techpaths* is a multimedia program designed to help teachers plan math instruction, have students practice on problems developed by teachers, and assess student work against exemplars that are aligned with National Council of Teachers of Mathematics (NCTM) and New York State's standards. It is a powerful instructional tool, but we made a mistake in introducing it as a new way to integrate technology into the curriculum. With a dozen teacher volunteers, the district organized three sessions in a computer lab where teachers could learn the software, examine the problems that are part of the program, and be supported in entering student work as part of the program's management system. Our approach was all wrong: Teachers started to look into the program but were overwhelmed by the job of choosing a specific problem to use with their class. They couldn't use the selection criteria effectively, and because they were working off a computer screen and didn't have hard copies of the problems, they couldn't page through and compare them. Teachers also reported that the program was too time-consuming to use. They already had a paper-and-pencil management system and felt that this was redundant. A few teachers used the program's feature to create new problems and extensions of problems, but only one attempted to incorporate them into the computer program.

As teachers revisited the program, they had questions about grouping for instruction, a process that can be managed through the use of the software. All these responses forced us to remember the purpose of introducing *Techpaths*: to support enhanced math instruction. Instead of focusing on how to integrate the technology into classroom practice, we had to look at student needs, student math, and then show how *Techpaths* could support our instructional effort. We now think of *Techpaths* as part of our math resource material, not as a stand-alone multimedia tool. In 1999–2000, we are using *Techpaths* as a source of three districtwide assessments. We are supporting teachers through their administration and scoring. The software helps us record, organize, and use the data to help students. In that way, *Techpaths* is a potential source of performance information that can be gathered in a systematic way to help round out the student achievement profiles the district is trying to develop. Learning from experiences like this raised new insights into the need for a different model of professional development to reflect our developing practices.

Professional Development

School reform efforts require as much support in their third year as in the first. After schools "tinker around the edges" by creating new master schedules or ordering new instructional materials, the hard work of actually changing practice really begins. This is as true in integrating technology into schools as in preparing for new state tests. For our system, that means a multifaceted approach to professional development with technology. Working closely with our teacher center (the Teacher Institute of Mamaroneck), we have offered a host of classes ranging from the use of graphing calculators to multi-media presentation software such as PowerPoint and Hyperstudio to Web-site design and Internet research. Stand-alone courses such as these are necessary, but they are insufficient.

To help people feel more comfortable with new approaches, the district has also tried to design a personalized approach to professional development. For example, in one school, teachers working on the development of digital portfolios were provided time during the summer to work with David Niguidula, a consultant from Providence, Rhode Island, who had done work in this area. The teachers involved in the portfolio project had experienced a number of frustrations. Their first efforts with prepackaged portfolio programs had been disappointing, particularly since the criteria in the packaged portfolios were not always consistent with what they valued in student work. Particularly in the primary grades, there was little place for the kinds of pictures and narratives characteristic of children for whom literacy is just emerging. In a second phase, when they developed their own portfolio guidelines, the sheer logistics were daunting. How much could young children scan or enter at the keyboard? Should the teacher enter the material after class time? Was the amount of effort required to gather the portfolio material worth the effort?

After a year of frustrating efforts to build portfolios during the school day, we provided time and support during the summer for the teachers to immerse themselves in the mechanics of the project and hone in on the ways they could most effectively integrate this project into their classroom practice. Even though progress was slow and frustration often high, the project taught us about professional development, as well as digital portfolios. For two years, the district hired Niguidula to meet with the teachers every two months to help them shape the portfolio project itself, work with them during the summer, and help define the kind of technological support they would need on an ongoing basis. This ongoing coaching has been an important component of the professional development plan. During this process, teachers partnered with each other and had students partnering with other students.

Another lesson from our work: The more we break the isolation of practice, the more successful the initiative. In this case, older students helping younger students was as important to the success of the digital portfolios as was the opportunity for teachers to support each other in this new classroom practice.

In another example of stretching our thinking about professional development, an elementary school worked with the Parent Teacher Association (PTA) to hire a technologist in residence, just as there were poets and writers in residence. Teachers felt that having a "techie" sitting by their side in the classroom could help build technological capacity within the school. In a third case, the district ran a set of workshops for the PTA on everything from publishing applications to Internet use, with a tutor for every two adults. In an effort to build on our understanding that the more personal the support, the more effective the transfer of new skills into practice, we planned a Superintendent's Conference Day that would demonstrate the ways technology supports the district's instructional priorities. Teachers from across the district volunteered to share their technology applications with other members of the staff. The format of the day was simple: Eight to ten teachers formed a group for a teacher presentation. During the morning, each teacher would see two ways their peers were using technology in the classroom. The presenters would gain by receiving feedback from the simple protocol for the morning (see Exhibit 3.1 for feedback form). The goal was to see technology as part of the ongoing work we do in classrooms. Just as teachers decide when to use cooperative learning or to engage in direct instruction, we hope that the use of technology will be deliberate in its intent and transparent in its delivery.

The Future

I think of school reform as requiring two lenses side by side. On one hand, we have to keep one lens focused sharply on the classroom, where the most important work of schools occurs. On the other hand, if we fail to look at the system, we cannot adequately support classroom practice or provide the kind of coherence that our students

Exhibit 3.1. Superintendent's Conference Day Reflections.

During and after each presentation you will be asked to write down your perspectives on each of five phases of the project. There will be an opportunity to share these comments with the presenters; your thoughts here should help you organize some ideas for the reflections phase of the exercise.

Presenting teacher(s) _____

Title of presentation _____

Phases	Questions I Have	What I Have Learned	What I Will Try
Purpose of the Presentation			
Description of the Presentation			
Setting			
• Description of students			
• Logistics of time and space			
Samples			
• Glimpses of student work			
• Ways to make student work visible			
Assessment			
• Ways in which activity is connected to assessment			

need. Thinking about technology is not different: We must focus our attention at the classroom and system level. Again, two specific initiatives in Mamaroneck illustrate efforts in both of these areas.

From the Classroom to the Boardroom

In a collaborative effort with the Mamaroneck Schools Foundation, the district will be funding two technologically rich elementary classrooms situated at opposite ends of the school district. In an action-research project with the Center for Children and Technology and Bena Kallick, an educational consultant to the district, we will try to identify some ways that technology can help students become more self-directed, self-monitoring learners, and we will explore the benefits to students when two teachers and many kids can collaborate in their learning. By marrying research to action where the "rubber hits the road"—the classroom—we hope that we can inform our practice across the district.

At the same time that we focus on the classroom, we must think about the district. The board struggles with questions of equity and access. Assuming that there are promising results from the technologically rich classrooms, there are financial and logistical challenges of how to scale up. While we will be trying to answer some of these questions as part of the action research project, the school system has already begun to explore a systems' perspective by engaging in IBM's Technology-Enriched Teaching and Learning Multi-District Project. The goal of this project is "to increase student success through the use of a systemic and data-driven approach to a comprehensive technology initiative for teaching and learning" (IBM project brochure). It requires asking a set of deceptively simple questions:

- What are the most effective areas of our current technology program?
- What can we learn from others about ways to improve our use of technology?

- How can we foster and maintain systemic and continuous improvement through the use of technology?
- How can we measure and report our progress within our schools and to the broader community?

By requiring that a district consider its technology program in the areas of communication; teaching and learning; planning and information management; organizational and professional development; access, reliability, and equity; and vision and leadership, this project supports a process by which a district can benchmark its work from the classroom to the boardroom. Furthermore, by asking that a district assess each indicator by looking at approach, implementation, and results, the system gains a full picture of the place of technology in the system.

Thoughts for Y2K

As a superintendent of schools, I have the recurring nightmare that technology will remain a glitzy show rather than a powerful tool to serve the larger mission of the district by supporting our need for information, communication, and building relationships on behalf of students.

The mission of our schools must remain primary: to engage students in work that requires them to use their minds well as they prepare to take their places as responsible citizens of a democratic society. With that as the end, we can use technology as a means, especially as we continue to increase our knowledge of its potential and refine and redefine the ways in which it can help us support our goals. In the end, we will not be measured by the ratio of computers to students or the multiple platforms we are able to support. Our work will be assessed by the way we have used technology to help us answer the only question that matters: How are our kids doing?

Chapter Four

Linking Technology to Educational Improvements

Jonathan P. Costa Sr., Esther Bobowick

"The journey of a thousand miles begins with one step." To begin to develop a process to think critically requires developing indicators of what currently is happening in the organization.

Now that the first wave of purchasing for technology and related infrastructure has hit schools, a second wave is building. This swell's landfall is related to its predecessor but has a different set of origins and consequences. The second wave is fueled by millions of dollars in computer spending and is composed of public constituencies who are about to request tangible evidence of improved student learning as a return on their substantial investments in technology.

Whether district leadership will ride the wave or drown in the surf depends on how well it has identified the purpose of integrating technology and to what extent it has developed indicators of success to measure it. The stakes are high because the dangers of going under are real. Without being able to provide a credible answer to the question of what is the impact on learning, support for the annual purchasing of hardware, which everyone knows is needed to keep technology alive as a viable tool for learning, will recede faster than a rip tide.

To help school communities deal with this issue, we have developed a technology self-assessment process (see Figure 4.1). Initiation of the process usually begins with the technology planning committee. The group uses the inventory of indicators (see Figure 4.2) as the

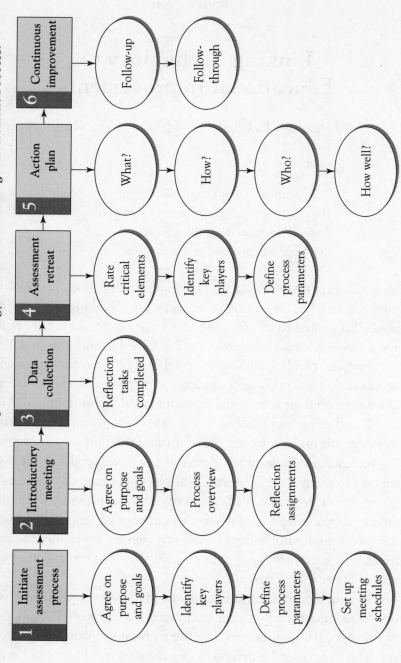

Figure 4.1. Determining the Impact of Technology on Student Learning: Assessment Process.

1 Initiate assessment process

- Agree on purpose and goals
- Identify key players
- Define process parameters
- Set up meeting schedules

2 Introductory meeting

- Agree on purpose and goals
- Process overview
- Reflection assignments

3 Data collection

- Reflection tasks completed

4 Assessment retreat

- Rate critical elements
- Identify key players
- Define process parameters

5 Action plan

- What?
- How?
- Who?
- How well?

6 Continuous improvement

- Follow-up
- Follow-through

Figure 4.2. Inventory and Scoring of Indicators.

Area of Focus	Rating
1. Systems and culture	0.00
2. Capacity	0.00
3. Instruction	0.00
4. Assessment	0.00
5. Curriculum	0.00

Overall Rating
0.00

Indicator Legend

Approach and planning indicators = ○
Implementation indicators = △
Results and performance indicators = □

1.1 Vision and planning
1.2 Systems thinking
1.3 Change leadership
1.4 Professional development
1.5 Culture and modeling
1.6 Fluency and literacy
1.7 Professional practice
2.1 Capacity
2.2 Networks and connectivity
2.3 Community and communication
2.4 Support
2.5 Management
2.6 Access and equity
3.1 Using standards
3.2 Engagement in learning
3.3 Motivation, relevance, and context
3.4 Higher-order thinking
4.1 Observable and reliable
4.2 Data collection process
4.3 Practical use
4.4 Access to assessment data
4.5 Deliverables and benchmarks
4.6 Improvement over time
5.1 Retention and application
5.2 Foundations
5.3 Continuous improvement
5.4 Links and connections
5.5 Leading to learn
5.6 Evidence

basis for gathering data. Each indicator is accompanied by a statement that further defines the indicator. For example, in Figure 4.3, indicator 1.1, vision and planning, is further explained with a scale that moves from the lowest rating (1)—"no statement of visions, unarticulated beliefs, disjointed or nonexistent plans, technical aspects only, exclusive"—to the highest rating (4)—"complete and descriptive, concise and compelling, interconnected and driving decisions, focused on learning, inclusive."

As a first lens on its work, the committee decides to whom the inventory will be given. For example, committee members may want to limit the survey to representatives from each building or they may want to extend the survey to all teachers and administrators. This early definition depends on the energy and resources of the committee. The decision made about who answers the survey determines the degree to which the committee can consider the survey a single source of reliable data.

The value of using this instrument is that it creates the first set of systematic observations about technology in a district. Given these measures, subsequent use of the instrument in the future can then provide the first set of "comparative" data and thereby offer the district a means to understand their progress or decline in numerous areas relevant to implementing technology.

The process of using this instrument mirrors the basic steps of strategic planning or the *feedback spiral:* agreement on purpose and key constituencies (steps one and two), collection of data and reflections on key indicators of performance (steps three and four), and then building improvement plans based on this information (steps five and six) (see Chapter One of this volume).

The fundamental purpose of promoting this process is to develop a set of indicators through which districts can measure progress in student learning. These indicators, however, have a dual purpose in also promoting the goals of integrating technology into the curriculum. So the first order of business in administering this assessment is to reaffirm or define a district's primary goals for using technology.

Figure 4.3. Survey of One Indicator.

1.1 Vision and Planning

A compelling vision and associated plan for the current and future use of technology for your schools should be developed and implemented. This vision and plan should be founded on an integration of technology strategy that is designed for the purpose of improved student learning for all members of the learning community.

1	2	3	4

No statement of vision	Complete and descriptive
Unarticulated beliefs	Concise and compelling
Disjointed or nonexistent plans	Interconnected and driving decisions
Technical aspects only	Focused on learning
Exclusive	Inclusive

Rationale for score:

Areas of district strength: Areas where growth is needed:

If you rated 2 or lower:

✓ Retreat for the purpose of vision building, technology planning, or some other process that will begin to forge a consensus on these critical issues.

4 Rethink the plan to tie every aspect of its scope and sequence to the improvement of student learning.

Most available research and practical experience suggest the following three reasons for investing in technology:

- To increase students' ability and interest in applying, in authentic settings, what districts and states have identified as learning and tasks that students should know and be able to do.

- To prepare students for success in a technology-centered world of work.

- To prepare students to manage and use information so they can be productive life-long learners and responsible citizens (*Education Week*, Oct. 1, 1998).

Once the final goals of a district are selected, there must be a direct relationship to student learning. District personnel must be able to provide reliable data that measure the influence of technology on student learning; otherwise, the most likely effect will be the reporting of standardized test scores in conjunction with some measure of technology "intensity" in the district (for example, computers per student) or technology expenditure.

This is a challenge because most school districts have few systemic approaches to measuring student achievement other than state or standardized tests. This dearth of measures can undermine efforts to identify the power of technology as a source of engagement, depth, and quality of learning and the opportunity for more students to demonstrate their knowledge. A self-assessment instrument can help a district determine whether it has a need for such additional measures.

A self-assessment tool of this sort can aid a district in the collection of data about student learning. To this end, we have identified twenty-nine indicators categorized by five broad areas of focus:

1. Systems and culture

    Vision and planning

    Systems thinking

    Change leadership

    Fluency and literacy

    Culture and modeling

    Access and equity

    Professional development

    Professional practice

    Management

2. Capacity

    Networks and connectivity

    Community and communication

    Support

3. Instruction
   Use of standards
   Engagement in learning
   Motivation, relevance, and context
   Higher-order thinking
4. Assessment
   Observability and reliability
   Practical use
   Deliverables and benchmarks
   Data collection process
   Decision making
   Access to assessment data
5. Curriculum
   Retention and application
   Foundations
   Results
   Assessment practices
   Leadership to learn
   Evidence
   Technology and improvement

The collection of data around these indicators follows the continuous improvement model of approach, implementation, and results. The *approach* phase asks questions about the process that a district is using to guide its work. *Implementation* asks questions regarding the degree to which we see it happening. *Results* looks for evidence that the approach and implementation has paid off in terms of increased student learning. Figure 4.2 presents an example of a form used in the assessment.

When administering this assessment instrument, participants are asked to think about their district's status in regard to each of the twenty-nine categories and score themselves based on a scale of one to four (Figure 4.3). A score of one would be given to demonstrate little or no evidence of the indicator present in the environment. At the other end of the scale, a score of four would demonstrate pervasive and systemic evidence of the indicator in the environment. Additionally, there is a narrative component that compels the participants to explain a rationale for the score, as well as to identify the areas of strength and weakness they discovered in the scoring process.

These assessment scores are then tabulated to produce individual indicators, area of focus, and overall district performance averages. Once all of the indicators are scored, a final data report is generated that provides baseline measures for understanding the status of technology in a district at a particular point in time.

In the first round, given the organizational benchmarks, these measures provide a foundation for a planning discussion that can begin to address questions such as, *In what areas are we in most need of improvement? On what specific indicators do we need to concentrate our efforts?* After a time, the self-assessment can be re-administered and used to guide the process of the feedback spiral, thus engaging the organization in a rational process of continuous learning.

From the initial diagnosis useful data can emerge. For example, the results of a report from a participating district (Figure 4.4) show that to improve its performance with technology and learning the district can examine how it measures, collects, and uses assessment information. On the basis of these results the group can then develop and implement improvement strategies that are directly tied to the district goals for learning and to its data-based measures of performance for those goals. In addition, it can redesign the instrument to gather further data about the success of the group's work. It can also design other data-gathering methods so that the district is continuously using data as a source for energizing its learning about the value of technology for improving student performance.

Experience with this instrument has shown that using these indicators and the supporting process provides users with three key benefits.

1. The first advantage is that they help to define—for district personnel, the board of education, and the community at large—the factors that have an impact on the district's technology

Figure 4.4. One District's Report on Technology Use.

Area of Focus	Rating
1. Systems and culture	2.57
2. Capacity	2.17
3. Instruction	3.25
4. Assessment	1.50
5. Curriculum	2.50

Overall Rating 2.40

1.1	Vision and planning	3	○
1.2	Systems thinking	2	○
1.3	Change leadership	3	○
1.4	Professional development	3	△
1.5	Culture and modeling	2	△
1.6	Fluency and literacy	3	□
1.7	Professional practice	2	□
2.1	Capacity	2	△
2.2	Networks and connectivity	2	△
2.3	Community and communication	2	△
2.4	Support	3	△
2.5	Management	2	△
2.6	Access and equity	2	△
3.1	Using standards	4	□
3.2	Engagement in learning	3	○
3.3	Motivation, relevance, and context	3	□
3.4	Higher-order thinking	3	□
4.1	Observable and reliable	2	□
4.2	Data collection process	1	○
4.3	Practical use	1	○
4.4	Access to assessment data	2	△
4.5	Deliverables and benchmarks	2	△
4.6	Improvement over time	1	□
5.1	Retention and application	3	□
5.2	Foundations	3	○
5.3	Continuous improvement	3	○
5.4	Links and connections	4	△
5.5	Leading to learn	1	△
5.6	Evidence	1	□

Indicator Legend

Approach and planning indicators = ○
Implementation indicators = △
Results and performance indicators = □

efforts. By clearly articulating the purposes of technology spending, a district can then work to improve on these purposes and measure its progress. Without such information, educators are left to wage the accountability battle unarmed.

2. Related to the first benefit, the second benefit of the instrument is that it creates a specific set of baseline accountability data that helps promote effective allocation of resources and focus efforts to improve.

3. Because the indicators used in this tool attempt to be systematic, the final benefit is that the results can provide information about a district's overall abilities to learn, grow, and achieve *regardless* of the use of technology. In fact, many of the items would be equally applicable if one was asking about the likelihood of any innovation taking hold and improving student learning.

The process of setting goals, understanding which indicators help to describe the implementation, measuring results toward meeting the goals, and using a self-assessment instrument to guide system change can be quite useful in promoting reasoned debate about the course of technology planning and expenditures. Using the methodology of the feedback spiral as a process for committee work will help discipline schools to see their work as a continuous act of studying, gathering data, and learning from the data to refine their work.

Once a district has completed this process it can then begin to address the question, *What is the impact on learning?* It will be able to identify more clearly any areas of weakness and track over time the progress of implementation plans that attempt to improve such conditions. Again, the intended result of engaging in this process is an increase in student learning and more effective leveraging of technology resources in the district toward that end.

With this accomplished, there will be only one thing left to do: grab the boards folks, the surf is up!

Reference

"Technology Counts." *Education Week*, Oct. 1, 1998.

Chapter Five

Using Technology to Promote Classroom Innovation

Kenneth C. Holvig, Gerald Crisci

How does technology change the process of
learning? The shift to design, research, and
simulation becomes central to students' acquisition
of knowledge.

Instruction in the "traditional" classroom revolves around the text-book, the blackboard, and the teacher. Information technology is changing this structure, and it is our experience that students are its greatest advocates. Students are leading the way in gathering information in new ways. Since they are comfortable with a digital environment, when presented with a research topic their first stop is usually their home Internet connection. They may do additional research in the library via traditional print resources. However, this research normally supplements what they consider to be their primary source of information—the Internet.

The Changing Pursuit of Knowledge

This shift presents a challenge to our teaching. Whereas we spent considerable time teaching students search techniques for the library, we now must also teach responsible search techniques for the Internet. Furthermore, we must coach students about the information they are finding by raising the following questions: Is this fact or opinion? Is this a reliable source? Is this written at an appropriate reading level for you? How might you cross-check your information with other sources to make certain that you have accounted for multiple perspectives?

With the advent of technology, the teacher has become a coach of critical thinking about what is gathered. Rather than assuming that all text is reliable, the student must analyze and synthesize the information and give meaning to the information.

We cannot accept students' reproducing what is written in the texts they research. If it was easy to copy the text and paraphrase in previous times, in the digital age it is altogether too easy to download and copy text right into the research paper. We now must frame the research question so that it requires students to take a stance, that is, offer their own interpretation of the material.

Technology-Enhanced Instruction: A New Model for Learning

Technology projects that allow students to be designers or participants in simulations engage students in tasks that can be powerful learning experiences. As one eighth grade student observes, "Technology has meaning for learning because it teaches us new ways to learn." These new ways to learn include design, simulation, and the enhanced resources and capabilities for research.

By offering our students opportunities to use simulations and to design and create, we are giving them practice in analysis, synthesis, and evaluation as they participate in problem solving. Massachusetts Institute of Technology professor Michael Dertouzos notes in his book *What Will Be,* "Sometimes we learn best by constructing rather than taking apart something we are trying to understand. 'Synthesis tools' or 'design tools' can help us learn through the design of real and virtual objects" (Dertouzos, 1997, p. 182). Teachers should seek to develop work that complements what technology has to offer. A technology-enhanced curriculum project has several characteristics that allow effective learning to take place.

How to Implement a Technology-Enhanced Curriculum Successfully

Implementing technology successfully requires the integration of a number of components.

Ask Appropriate Questions. Questions need to be framed in light of concepts rather than facts. They should require the student to evaluate multiple sources of information to construct meaningful conclusions. For example, asking students to write a report on the broad topic of humpback whales does not provide students with an opportunity to engage in thoughtful research by using information technology. A better project would be to ask them to write about how whaling has changed through the years, or if a certain species of whale should be protected and why they think so. In other words, students must take a position with their findings. In so doing, they can harness the power of the Internet by getting a more current and global perspective on the question.

Create Opportunities for Students to Use Different Media. Given the powerful multimedia and programming capability of computers, students may choose to design Web pages, multimedia presentations, or desktop published documents to exhibit their technical skills and understanding of the curriculum. In these cases teachers act as facilitators, helping students structure their projects while helping them meet goals. Students have the opportunity to reflect on the appropriateness of their choices in developing such projects in terms of the choice of media, the form of presentation, and the content. Such activities are best guided by rubrics that help students understand the criteria by which to judge such choices.

Exploit Technology's Capability for Group Projects. There are many opportunities for teamwork in using technology. By working in teams, students have the opportunity to participate in valuable cooperative learning experiences. Students take on roles to share in the planning, decision making, and construction of their projects. This type of environment supports the "design studio" model of instruction, in which students collaborate on projects.

Provide Opportunities to Learn Along the Way. Oftentimes, teachers assign projects as homework and miss the valuable opportunity to teach students how to work their way through a project to a high-quality end. When projects are given sufficient classroom teaching time and instruction is focused on higher-level thinking skills, students are pressed to think their way through complex material. Many teachers ask students to practice skills as their homework so that they can devote more classroom time to coaching for better thinking. This implies fewer projects of greater depth and significance. In addition, students are asked to reflect and assess their work. Through directed instruction regarding planning, time management, accessing, processing, and communicating learning, students are working in the authentic ways that work is done outside of school.

Promote Interdisciplinary Projects. Effective technology projects draw from a variety of curriculum areas. The world outside of school is not compartmentalized into disciplines. When one is trying to understand the economy, one must know about the social context in which the economy rests: What is the government? How does the education system work? What religious orientations are a significant part of the culture? Therefore, it is important for students to learn how to make cross-disciplinary connections. For example, third-grade students examine math patterns in nature. They learn how to use computer tools to design a flower. First students create a flower petal. Then they learn how to spin the petal to create a realistic flower pattern. As students move into fourth grade, they learn to create snowflakes by using the same technique. First they design one "branch" of the snowflake, then they learn to rotate it to create a snowflake pattern. The connections among math, science, and art become more apparent to students as they engage in these design-based activities. Again, although this could be done with paper and a stencil, the technology makes such a project that combines geometry, biology, esthetics, and design much more accessible and easier to deploy by the teacher—and far more enjoyable for the pupil.

Use Technology Appropriately. Technology serves an important function in supporting the curriculum, but it should not always be at "center stage." Sound pedagogy dictates that decisions are made about when to use computers and when not to use them on the basis of what the desired learning outcomes are. Students need to learn how to make wise choices about when it is appropriate to use the Internet, for example, and when it would be more appropriate to go to the library and use maps or other, more traditional sources readily available.

Barriers to Implementing a Technology-Enhanced Curriculum

The changes we've discussed are a challenge and do not come easily. A number of institutional barriers must be considered as well in attempting to implement a technology-enhanced curriculum successfully.

Faced with the constraints of a period schedule, the physical space, the budget process, and the organization of students, teachers may find it difficult to move toward this new teaching model. By identifying these constraints and raising the awareness of school officials, teachers may help to effect the kinds of changes needed to extend and transform the curriculum with technology. Common problems include inadequate AC power, lack of outside phone access, and inappropriate seating and work space. Whatever the problem, school officials must be willing to work with teachers and the school community to make the necessary changes.

Human Resources: The Changing Role of the Teacher

To work within this new technology-enhanced classroom effectively, teachers must develop new coaching skills. Additionally, they must exhibit

- A level of comfort with technology
- A willingness to learn with the students
- Flexibility with time and scheduling
- A willingness to accept more self-directed learning

We have witnessed a change in our approach to teaching, with the advent of technology, here in Scarsdale. We have applauded a number of teachers at all levels who have exhibited the characteristics of the facilitator. Although they occasionally use prepackaged programs, these teachers are more likely to provide their students with *tool-based* software to construct their own learning.

Our students have engaged in a number of projects that use this type of software. For example:

- Sixth grade students create multimedia book reports with HyperStudio. Unlike traditional written reports, these presentations come alive on the screen with hypertext, video, sound, and Internet links—all valuable technology skills to learn.
- Fifth grade students take part in a project called Pinball Math. The project involves the creation of interactive computer pinball games that incorporate a variety of mathematical concepts.
- Students use MicroWorlds Logo, a mathematically rich programming environment to create their games. The project helps students integrate many programming and math concepts and often leads students to go beyond the structure of a traditional "pinball" game. Some children create sports games (hockey, soccer, and basketball); others create games with themes based on a unit studied in school (acid rain).

The Nagging Doubts: Does Technology Really Matter?

The possibilities offered by technology seem endless. However, the many challenges of implementing technology have many of us wondering, Does it really matter in terms of student performance? An important voice in this concern is the voice of the student.

Empowerment. Whatever they create, students realize how technology empowers them. For example, upon completing a sophisticated, interactive program, one fifth grade girl exclaimed, "Wow! I did this with a friend—all by myself, not someone older than me, *I did this*. It's a big shock."

Engagement. A seventh grader observes, "When you read out of a textbook, a lot of information is given that teachers expect you to learn. The problem with this is that we do not want to learn the material in such a boring manner."

By using technology, especially the Internet and multimedia, students can learn the same information in many different ways. If the student may choose which way is easiest for him or her, the learning will follow naturally and efficiently.

Authenticity. Whether their access is in the classroom, the computer lab, or at home, students have formed their opinions about technology. In a poll of one hundred eighth graders, we learned that students view technology as a key to future success. One student notes, "Learning how to use the tools of technology will allow us to have more success later in our lives. In the future, technology may run the world. So everybody should know something about it."

Another student agrees. "Technology is a big part of the future, and children today are the future leaders of the world. So the students must learn how to use technology, and everything about it, so they can apply it later in life."

As technology-using teachers, we believe what these students say. But do we have hard evidence to support the notion that technology does improve learning? In a recent article in *Learning and*

Leading with Technology, editor David Moursund wrestles with the question, "Is information technology improving education?" He notes, "Business has spent far more per capita than education to support employee use of information technology, and business is still questioning the effectiveness of this investment. It is not surprising that education lacks solid evidence that this aspect of information technology improves the productivity of students and educators" (Moursund, 1997, p. 5).

Solid evidence may be just down the hallway at Scarsdale Middle School where eighth-grade social studies teacher Joe Cesarano rewrote his curriculum to make technology the main tool for learning. Each student has daily access to a networked computer. Joe carefully observes his students and has, in essence, become a researcher experimenting with the effective use of information technology in the classroom (see Chapter Six). It is not surprising that when asked about the impact of technology on his learning, one of Joe's eighth graders said, "Technology has opened a new and better window for learning." It seems Joe's students have reflected on the meaning of technology for their learning.

Steps to Bringing Technology to Scale: Moving from Labs to Classrooms

Joe's approach works in our current school configuration because his is the exception, not the rule. He has computers in his classroom. If every teacher in the school were to have the same, we would not be able to meet the demand for computers. We are encouraged with laptops and portable digital assistants becoming more affordable, since that development may help with the necessary resource allocation for our building. We presently rely heavily on computer labs for our students, although we recognize that "just-in-time" learning takes place best in the classroom, where technology may be one of many tools available for the task. At this point in our school's development, parents, teachers, and administration are not ready to give up the security of the computer lab, with an assigned computer teacher, for a classroom-based system.

This move is substantial, as it is both costly and will truly alter the classroom. When more definitive data arrive about the link between technology and learning, and it is positive, then the possibility of that evolution will be palpable. If the news is positive, then the nagging doubts will subside and with it many barriers.

What Have We Learned About Implementing Technology?

A number of important issues will emerge as educators plan for the inevitable changes they will encounter as the technology revolution continues to gain momentum. Our practice reinforces the following necessary steps we must pursue as we build our school into a true learning organization.

- Engage in strategic planning as an ongoing part of the learning rather than as a "five-year" plan. Technology changes too rapidly to consider five years at a chunk. Districts must engage in strategic planning that addresses the potential impact of technology in order to avoid jumping on the latest technology bandwagon (see Chapter Four).
- Create a cycle of learning specifically related to the plan (see Chapter One).
- Provide staff development opportunities that are rich with experience and just-in-time learning for teachers so they can see the advantages and problems of working in that context (see Chapter Eight). Schools must invest in meaningful staff development opportunities for all teachers that go beyond simply developing technical proficiency.
- Focus on student growth and learning. Continue the search for best practices based on the performance of students in a technology-rich environment (see Chapter Seven).

- Address equity issues to ensure that all students have access to computers and other powerful educational resources.

As the use of technology continues to improve and becomes more accessible for students and teachers, we believe and hope that schools will be transformed from isolated classrooms into vibrant learning communities. If technology can promote this, then surely technology matters.

References

Dertouzos, M. *What Will Be*. New York: Harper Collins, 1997.
Moursund, D. "Is Information Technology Improving Education?" *Learning and Leading with Technology*, 1997, 26(4), 4–5.

Chapter Six

Learning About Technology Through Action Research

Barbara Schain Spitz, Madge Hildebrandt Klais

> The process of action research cultivates a method
> whereby educators can reflect on their practices.

Action research offers a process to support teachers as they reflect on their current practices. The reflections often guide their thinking in making wiser and more informed decisions about what is important. As part of the action research process, teachers identify a meaningful question that directly relates to their own classroom practices and experiences. Collecting, organizing, analyzing, and reflecting on the data helps teachers assess their work and then consider ways of doing things differently. When action research is used as a method for studying the effects of technology, it can serve as a catalyst for restructuring teaching and learning.

How do teachers begin an action research project? They often begin with a curriculum design or an experiment with instruction that integrates the use of technology. The primary concern is learning; technology is a tool to promote higher performance from students.

Through action research, teachers often are inspired to develop entirely new classroom environments, where learning becomes more collaborative, interactive, and customized. Action research also provides knowledge to others in the organization. For example, the research project presented in this book is part of a collection of research articles produced by the Madison, Wisconsin, Metropolitan School District. In Chapter Seven, Madge Hildebrandt Klais, Sherman Middle School librarian in Madison, Wisconsin, examines her current teaching practices and asks, "How can electronic information access skills be effectively taught to young adolescents?" Hildebrandt Klais relates her decision to abandon her old practices of teaching individual students how to use specific electronic indexes and describes her new approach, which is first to focus on teaching basic information and library skills and concepts through exploring the telephone book as a model database. She then plans to have students practice a variety of strategies for accessing information. With that basic database concept and understanding, Hildebrandt Klais anticipates that students can make an informed and smoother transition from the telephone book to the computer catalog and electronic indexes.

Chapter Seven reveals the power of action research. The issues and questions under consideration are personal and focused on Hildebrandt Klais's teaching practices. Her data collection is focused on student achievement and student attitude. Upon analyzing the student outcomes, she concludes that direct teaching of library information skills, beginning with the telephone book as a model database and then moving to electronic indexes, is more effective than her previous practices of individually teaching students how to use the technology first. The process results in the author's becoming better informed about her teaching practices and empowered to make more thoughtful decisions about the integration of technology tools into her curriculum.

Stories about action research in the classroom provide the educational community with important information about teaching and learning with technology tools. Teachers' experiences as researchers have great value. Their observations, reflections, and writings are primary sources of knowledge about classroom practices. The action research process opens up teachers to change and reflection. Cathy Caro-Bruce, a staff and organization development specialist in the Madison school district, reports that over three hundred teachers in the district have participated in action research. Caro-Bruce reports that many teachers indicate "participation in the program helped them develop more confidence in their ability as teachers to influence their work and the circumstances in which they practice."

Chapter Seven

Teaching Computer Search Skills to Middle School Students

Madge Hildebrandt Klais

> Students need skills to navigate the electronic
> universe of data, information, and knowledge
> successfully.

Today students are faced with a powerful medium for accessing information, the Internet. However, to use the Internet effectively requires research skills for searching among many electronic documents. Teaching the skill of searching is precisely what librarians have to offer. It is an interdisciplinary skill that now has an electronic universe of data, information, and knowledge to which to apply itself.

I am the only teacher at Sherman Middle School who has to "borrow" students in order to do my job. As the school librarian, I am charged with teaching young adolescents how to locate, comprehend, evaluate, and apply information found within and through the library media center (LMC), but there exists no formal program for achieving these goals. However, I am not alone in my predicament: Schools and school librarians who follow the national guidelines for library media programs seek to integrate the teaching of what have traditionally been called "library skills" into the total school curriculum. We strive to work with teachers to incorporate skill instruction into specific classroom activities and projects by using a model of flexible scheduling. Having abandoned a rigid schedule of weekly library classes, we now schedule classes into the LMC when library experiences and instruction appear appropriate for the research requirements of those classes. Flexible scheduling is thus designed to ensure that library instruction is authentic—that students learn skills that fulfill a real and immediate need. Otherwise, skills learned in isolation and with no clear practical application or reinforcement in the classroom are quickly lost and require reteaching.

Although most librarians endorse this ideal of flexible scheduling and integration of the library media curriculum, the reality of our school day often inhibits our ability to reach the ideal. Not all teachers understand the need for library skills instruction. And even when teachers are eager to include the library in their curriculum, it is difficult to carve out mutually convenient planning times when teacher(s) and librarian can meet to construct an appropriate library unit or activity. Furthermore, teaching library skills at the same time that students are working on a specific research project can often be more distracting than helpful. How, then, given the constraints of the typical school setting, can library information skills and concepts be effectively taught, given the broader resources available when using electronic media?

This is the question that I posed for myself as I embarked on my fourth year as the LMC director (librarian) at Sherman Middle School. Although I have always been an enthusiastic supporter of the teaching goals set forth by the American Association of School Librarians, I have been frustrated in my attempts to reach those goals. Because I must rely on the cooperation of classroom teachers, I have never been able to include all Sherman students in formal skills instruction, nor have I been sure that the students who participated in formal skills instruction learned those skills well or continued to apply them during their career at Sherman. Therefore, my goal for this classroom action research project has been to evaluate the effectiveness of library media skill instruction at Sherman.

However, I did not attempt in this study to include instruction in all library information skills but chose to focus on skills related to the use of electronic indexes. I chose this focus because teaching students how to use computerized indexes is the purview primarily of the school library media specialist. Unlike other information and research skills, electronic information access skills can be taught and assessed by the school librarian without extensive planning or teaming with a classroom teacher. Furthermore, computerized catalogs and indexes are a relatively new addition to school libraries, and few standards or commercial programs exist to help guide the school librarian in this instruction. Being able to search electronic indexes for information requires skills somewhat different from those required to search a card catalog or a paper index. To date, only a few studies have examined how students master these skills compared to how they master nonelectronic information access skills. Since Sherman Middle School does not even own a card catalog, I decided that our students would benefit most from an investigation of the question, *How can electronic information access skills be effectively taught to young adolescents?*

History

When Sherman Middle School opened in the fall of 1991, the staff looked forward to establishing a model educational program for young adolescents. Each year for three years, we added one grade level. Because of the relative newness of Sherman and the continuing experimentation with student groupings and curriculum, our school is in a state of flux. We also have had to contend with a large amount of yearly staff turnover as well as with a challenging school population. Nearly half of our students read below grade level as measured by standardized achievement tests. Forty percent of our students qualify for free lunches or reduced-cost lunches. In addition, 17 percent of the Sherman population are special needs students (cognitively disabled, learning disabled, emotionally disabled, and those requiring speech and language instruction), and these students are fully integrated into the regular instructional program.

The Sherman Library Media Center

It is not my purpose here to analyze Sherman's successes and problems but rather to describe the school setting for the library media center and to introduce elements of the school program that influence the continuing development of the library media program and instruction in information access skills specifically. As Sherman grew in one-year increments, so did the LMC. Our school is housed in an old building that had been used for twelve years for nonpublic school activities, and it required renovation before re-opening in 1991. The LMC underwent the most extensive renovation in the building in anticipation of incorporating computer hardware and other audio-visual equipment. We purchased library resources in three one-year phases and completed most of the acquisitions last year.

This collection and building effort was, of necessity, my first priority, and this is the first year that I have had the time and resources to focus on building an information skills curriculum. Because of the large turnover of staff at Sherman (at the end of the last school year, we lost one-third of our teaching staff), it has been difficult to provide continuity to the program from one year to the next. Because I need to "borrow" students to teach them, it is necessary to build bridges to their teachers to develop long-term goals for skills acquisition. With so many staff members leaving Sherman, this has been a particularly challenging aspect of my job.

Orientation Stations

For the first two years of Sherman's existence, I taught information skills (for examples of information skills, see Exhibit 7.1) to individual students as the need arose or in conjunction with a classroom research project. During the third year, when Sherman had all three grades on board for the first time, I implemented an individualized information skills program that I dubbed *orientation stations* (thanks to Judy Patrick for suggesting the title). Teachers contracted with me to bring their classes to the LMC for a week. Older students were paired with younger students to explore six-

Exhibit 7.1. Electronic Information Access Concepts and Skills.

Concepts

Data	Index	Bibliography	Boolean
Database	Source	Call number	connectors
Information	Keyword	Dewey Decimal	(operators)
retrieval	Entry	System	
Access	Citation	CD-ROM	

Skills

Able to conduct a subject search

Able to conduct a keyword search

Able to articulate the difference between a subject search and a keyword
search

Able to conduct a Boolean search

Able to write a citation for a book, magazine article, and newspaper article

Able to determine the appropriate source and index for finding specific
information (book, magazine, newspaper)

Able to create a bibliography of appropriate sources

Able to summarize the main points covered by a particular source (create
an abstract)

teen stations that I had set up in the library. Each pair of students
was required to complete a worksheet for each station. The work-
sheets posed a question to be answered by using the index or source
at that station and also demanded that the students reflect on the
research process they had used to find the answer. I introduced this
activity by demonstrating how to work at a sample station. Stations
included the computer catalog for the LMC collection, electronic
newspaper and magazine indexes, atlases, encyclopedias, and
almanacs. At the end of the week, students were tested individually (not with their partner) on their knowledge of the indexes and
sources and their ability to locate information.

Overall, the results were disappointing. Seventh-grade and
eighth-grade students who had had previous exposure to these
resources performed much better than students who had never used
the Sherman LMC. It was apparent that rather than teaching

sixth-grade students how to use the resources, the older students were doing most of the work themselves. Furthermore, the older students exhibited many gaps in their knowledge and understanding of information skills. However, only one teacher brought her class back to the library for further skills instruction and testing. Nearly 50 percent of her class had failed the posttest. To ensure that all of them had acquired a basic understanding of library skills and procedures, they came in groups of three to five students to work directly with me on mastering the orientation stations. They determined when they thought they were ready to take another posttest, and every student was required to work on skills in the LMC until he or she could pass the test. All students eventually succeeded.

Although all students in a single class achieved mastery, this method of skills acquisition proved to be very inefficient and time-consuming. Had all eight teachers whose students had participated in orientation stations contracted with me to work with small groups until they achieved 100 percent success, I would not have had any time left to perform all my other library duties. It became clear to me that I needed to rethink information skills instruction at Sherman Middle School.

Description of This Study

This school year (1994–1995) I abandoned the individualized, orientation stations concept and introduced a directed teaching program for sixth and seventh-graders. Rather than focus exclusively on how to use specific indexes and resources, I began by teaching basic information and library skills and concepts (see Exhibit 7.1). Students learned these by exploring the telephone book as a model database and practicing a variety of strategies for accessing information. They then moved from the telephone book to the computer catalog for our media collection and then to electronic indexes for accessing newspaper and magazine articles (for information on the specific hardware and software used for this study, see Exhibit 7.2). Although the focus of the program was electronic indexes, students

Exhibit 7.2. Software and Hardware Used in the Sherman Middle School Study.

Software

- Computer catalog: *Search Plus*, Follett Software Company, 1391 Corporate Drive, McHenry, Illinois 60060–7041

- Newspaper index: NewsBank Electronic Index (electronic index with full text on microfiche), NewsBank, Inc., 58 Pine Street, New Canaan, Connecticut 06840–5426

- Magazine index: WILSONDISC (Electronic index with abstracts for most entries), H.W. Wilson Co., 950 University Avenue, Bronx, New York 10452

- Combined magazine and newspaper index: SIRS Researcher (Electronic index with full text articles), Social Issues Resources Series, P.O. Box 2348, Boca Raton, Florida 33487–2348

Hardware

All four indexes are available on a Novell local area computer network. Three computers on this network are 286 IBM machines, and six computers on this network are Dell 486 machines. The computer catalog alone is also available on a Model 25 IBM machine. Three of the Dell machines are used for LMC management tasks and are not normally available for student use. We are in the process of replacing all the IBM machines with 486 computers that have at least eight megabytes of RAM.

To run these indexes, we use a CD-ROM tower and server that is connected to the LMC server. The LMC server is, in turn, connected to the school server, and most classrooms can access the LMC server on their 286 IBM machines. As we upgrade the LMC computing capacity, we will find the classroom computers less useful because they will not have adequate memory to drive some of the new CD-ROM applications that we will be adding to the LMC tower.

also spent some time learning about the resources available in the reference collection, both in paper and computer format.

Questions Posed for the Study

I hoped that by implementing this new program, I would be able to more effectively and efficiently teach information skills than I had previously been able to do at Sherman. My overall study question was, *How can electronic information access skills be effectively taught to young adolescents?* To answer this question, I posed a series of sub-questions as well:

- How can electronic information skills be taught when there are a limited number of computers available in the LMC?
- Can students with impaired language arts skills (underachievers) learn and employ these skills and concepts?
- How should instruction in information skills be related to general classroom instruction?
- Does formal instruction in information skills enhance student attitudes toward the library (and behavior in the library)?
- What can be learned from this study that may have broader application to teaching young adolescents?

During the last decade, the installation of computers in school libraries has altered the nature of skills instruction and placed some constraints on the physical capacity of the LMC to accommodate whole-class instruction. That is, when basic information access skills were taught using the card catalog, most students in a given class of twenty to thirty students could receive immediate hands-on experience with the index to the library collection because each student could explore a single catalog drawer. With the advent of computerized catalogs and indexes, it became impossible to provide hands-on experience to an entire class at the same time. Even with networked computers such as we have in the Sherman LMC, the capacity to provide hands-on information access experience is severely reduced.

Since the configuration of computer placement throughout a school varies from school to school, each library media specialist must tailor skills instruction that is viable in his or her unique school setting. At Sherman, we have eight computer stations that access the collection catalog and seven that also provide access to electronic indexes to magazine and newspaper articles. If the need arises, we can sometimes use three LMC management computers that are also on our library network. To provide hands-on experience to students receiving skills instruction, we can accommodate seven to eight students individually or fourteen to sixteen students working in pairs. Although staff and students can access the LMC computer network in their classrooms, most rooms are equipped with only one computer, thus rendering the schoolwide network useless for whole-class instruction. In addition, our school houses a networked computer laboratory equipped with Macintosh computers that are not accessible from the library or the classroom. We have been forced, therefore, to rethink the old paradigm of whole-class skills instruction.

Class Composition

During the first semester, I used my newly developed program with three classes of combined sixth and seventh-graders. For the second semester, I worked with two classes of combined sixth and seventh-graders. These were all heterogeneously grouped classes. Although the same program was followed with all the students, it differed in some details from class to class.

The first time that I taught the program, I contracted with two teachers, Nancy Engle and Jim Lister, to teach information access skills to all their students during the first quarter of the school year. This library program became one component of a language arts rotation of small groups of students. Each day for four days of every week, a different group of ten to twelve students came to the LMC for forty minutes of instruction, so each group of students worked with me one day a week in the LMC. Each week, I introduced a new lesson that built upon the work of the previous week (see Exhibit 7.3). Each lesson began with an activity that we completed as a whole group, followed by a similar activity that the students practiced individually. These assignments were handed in for pass-fail credit. The students were given a test during the ninth week that consisted of two basic parts: a verbal (or conceptual) exam

Exhibit 7.3. Introduction to Databases: The Telephone Book.

1. What does the word *data* mean?
2. What does the word *retrieval* mean?
3. What is a *database?*
4. Why is the telephone book a *database?*
5. What other kinds of *databases* do you have at home or in your classroom?
6. What is an *index?*
7. Why is the telephone book an *index?*
8. What sort of *data* are *indexed* in the telephone book?
9. What information in the telephone book is *not* arranged alphabetically?
10. On what page in the phone book do you find the name Ingvarr Suvorov?
11. If you needed to find the phone number of a pet cemetery, in what section of the phone book would you look? On what page would you find it?
12. In what section of the phone book would you find the phone number for the restaurant called The Blue Marlin? On what page would you find it?
13. What is the zip code for Harbor House Drive in Madison?
14. What did you learn about the telephone book today that you did not already know?

that assessed the ability of the students to explain in written form the skills and concepts they had learned, and a functional exam that asked students to locate information in the LMC by using a variety of strategies (see Exhibit 7.4). They also filled out an evaluation of the experience (see Exhibit 7.5). At the same time that these students were learning information skills, they were also practicing them while they worked on miniresearch projects with their classroom teachers.

A third teacher, Cindy Barbera, requested that I teach the same program to her sixth and seventh-grade students during the second quarter of the school year. This unit replicated the one used with the previous two classes.

Exhibit 7.4. Information Skills Posttests.

Posttest One

(Used with Engle, Lister, and Barbera Classes)

1. Why is the telephone book a *database?*
2. How does an *index* work?
3. Name two *databases* in the LMC that are also *indexes:*
   a.
   b.
4. In what section of the telephone book would you find phone numbers for stores that sell vacuum cleaners?
5. What information is listed in the white pages of the telephone book?
6. Why is the computer catalog an *index?*
7. What is a *keyword* used for?
8. Give one example of a *source* of information in the library.
9. What *database* is used for locating newspaper articles in the library?
10. How are newspaper articles stored in the library?

Posttest Two

(Used with Grau and Gil Casado Classes)

Part I: Short Answer

1. List three ways in which a telephone book and the computer catalog are alike:
   a.
   b.
   c.
2. What is NEWSBANK used for?
3. How are WILSONDISC and SIRS different?
4. What three connecting words are used in a Boolean search?
5. What is the Dewey Decimal System?
6. When you write a citation for a book, what five pieces of information should you include?
   a.
   b.
   c.
   d.
   e.

(Continued)

Exhibit 7.4. Continued.

7. What is the difference between a subject search and a keyword search on the computer catalog?

8. Why is it important to include a bibliography when you write a report?

9. Name two kinds of sources that you can find in the reference section of the library:

   a.

   b.

10. What reference book did you review for our "book share"?

Part II: Writing an Abstract

Read a newspaper article. Write an abstract of what you have read in the space below.

Part III: Demonstrate How You Can Find Information in the LMC

Get an index card with a test question from Ms. Hildebrandt Klais. When you find the answer to the question on the card, fill out the answer space below. Be sure to include the number of the question that you answered as well as the complete answer to the question. You may use any source in the LMC except a person.

For the third quarter, Debra Gil Casado and Bryan Grau contracted with me to teach information access skills to their students. I followed the same program as during the first semester, but this time I worked with students for two consecutive class periods a week. Students were separated into groups of twelve to fifteen sixth-graders and twelve to fifteen seventh-graders and received instruction separately by grade level. Because the students received nearly twice as much instruction during the nine-week period, I expanded the program to include not only accessing information but also creating bibliographies and summarizing the content of sources they had located. The topics used for searching information were often related to topics of study in the students' classroom work. As in the case of the previous units, these students took a posttest and filled out an evaluation of the program. For the last

Exhibit 7.5. Information Skills Evaluation.

Evaluation One

Used with Engle, Lister, and Barbera classes)

Please circle the number that best matches your opinion:

1. Finding information in the telephone book was

5	4	3	2	1
very easy	easy	difficult	very difficult	

2. Finding information in the computer catalog was

5	4	3	2	1
very easy	easy	difficult	very difficult	

3. What I liked *best* about learning library skills was:

4. What I liked *least* about learning library skills was:

5. I could have used more help with:

6. This is how I usually behaved during the library skills activities:

7. If I could change anything about the skills activities, this is what I would change:

Evaluation Two

(Used with Grau and Gil Casado classes)

Please circle the number that best matches your opinion:

1. Finding information in the computer catalog was

5	4	3	2	1
very easy	easy	difficult	very difficult	

2. Finding information in other electronic indexes was

5	4	3	2	1
very easy	easy	difficult	very difficult	

3. What I liked *best* about learning library skills was:

4. What I liked *least* about learning library skills was:

5. I could have used more help with:

6. This is how I usually behaved during the library skills activities:

7. If I could change anything about the skills activities, this is what I would change:

quarter of the school year, all the seventh-grade students from these two classes continued to visit the LMC three days a week to work on an independent study project that required them to implement the skills they had learned during the previous quarter.

Data Collection

Data on student achievement and attitudes were collected in a variety of ways. The posttest was the primary instrument for assessing achievement, supplemented by the informal observations of the library media specialist and the classroom teachers. Daily assignments also provided an indicator of student progress. Written student evaluations as well as the observations of the librarian and the classroom teachers were used to assess student attitudes toward the instruction.

Student Outcomes—Achievement

The following observations about student achievement are based on the results of the posttest:

- All students in all five classes, with the exception of one cognitively disabled student and one student for whom English is a second language, passed the functional portion of the exam. That is, after the instructional program, these students were all able to perform simple subject, author, and title searches on the electronic indexes.
- Students with significant deficiencies in language arts skills performed less well on the verbal or conceptual part of the test, but they all passed the overall test because of their good performance on the functional part of the test.
- In every class where the students were taught in combined grades (Lister, Engle, Barbera), the seventh-graders on average scored higher on the posttest than the sixth-graders.
- In Cindy Barbera's class, all of the seventh-graders who had received additional instruction in orientation stations last

year as sixth-graders scored highly on this posttest. They all earned A's with the exception of one seventh-grader with severe behavioral problems and another who is reading below grade level.

- In the two classes where the students were taught separately by grade, students' test performance was similar on average. That is, sixth-graders tended to perform as well or better than their seventh-grade classmates.

- I have subsequently observed that most of the students who received this skill instruction have continued to employ the skills they learned and are more independent library users than the students who have had no formal instruction to develop information access skills at Sherman. The students from the Grau and Gil Casado classrooms have been especially skilled at using all the electronic indexes during the two months since completing their instruction.

Student Outcomes—Attitude

Student attitudes toward this instruction may be summarized as follows:

- The written evaluations by students were intended to be anonymous, so there was no means of determining whether the responses were those of sixth or seventh-graders for the classes of combined students. The perception of most students in those classes was that finding information in the telephone book and the computer catalog was "easy" to "very easy"; more students responded that finding information in the telephone book was "very easy" than responded that finding information in the computer catalog was "very easy."

- Because more time had been spent with the separately taught classes (Grau and Gil Casado) on instructing students on how to use other electronic indexes in addition to the computer catalog, the evaluation instrument was altered slightly to reflect this change. Students were asked to assess the difficulty of using the computer catalog and the electronic indexes and were not asked their opinion of the difficulty of using the telephone book. For both the sixth and seventh-graders, finding information in the computer catalog was perceived to be slightly easier than finding information in other electronic indexes.

- In both the Grau and Gil Casado classes, many more sixth-graders than seventh-graders perceived finding information in electronic indexes, including the computer catalog, to be less than "easy" (although not downright "difficult") than did seventh-graders.

- Although no question on the student evaluations directly asked the students their opinion of the instruction, the final question of the survey may be an indirect measure of how the students felt about the instruction. The instrument states, "If I could change anything about the skills activities, this is what I would change." The majority of students in all classes either responded "nothing" or left the answer blank. Although these responses may not be a ringing endorsement of the program, they also indicate a lack of serious dissatisfaction with it.

- As the library media specialist and sole teacher of these lessons, I observed that students came willingly to the library for instruction and seldom complained about the program as a whole or individual lessons. The students exhibited most enthusiasm for the hands-on computer activities and the "treasure hunt"-type of information searches.

Findings

Upon analyzing the student outcomes, I concluded that direct teaching of library information skills was more effective than the individualized, peer-teaching method of instruction (orientation stations) that I employed during the previous school year. Specific answers to the questions posed for this study are as follows:

1. How can electronic information skills be taught when a limited number of computers are available in the LMC?

   These skills can only be taught to groups of students when every student or every two students can be given immediate access to a computer. In the case of Sherman Middle School, this means that the LMC can accommodate no more than half a class for skills instruction.

   One positive result of the limited number of computers is that teachers can divide their classes in half, thereby dramatically reducing the pupil-teacher ratio. I taught students alone in the LMC while teachers worked on another activity in the classroom with the other half of their class.

2. Can students with impaired language arts skills (underachievers) learn and employ these skills and concepts?

   Yes. However, instruction should be coupled with ongoing language arts instruction. Most of these students had difficulty conducting Boolean searches. They often stopped their library research when they found the sources of information, and they were reluctant to read or use the sources they found.

3. How should instruction in information skills be related to general classroom instruction?

   For sixth-graders, library skills are most effectively taught when they are separated from a specific research project. Skills can be tied to regular classroom instruction by using examples of topics currently under study in the classroom or by prefacing a research project with skills instruction. Skills may then be reinforced during the research project.

4. Does formal instruction in information skills enhance student attitudes toward the library (and behavior in the library)?

Although the results of the attitude surveys were inconclusive, my observations led me to believe that students developed positive attitudes toward the library as a result of skills instruction. I also observed improved student behavior because I was able to build relationships with students through skill instruction in a way that I am unable to do through a "hit-or-miss" or "catch-as-catch-can" approach to skills instruction.

5. What can be learned from this study that may have broader application to teaching young adolescents?

Teachers should carefully examine the effect of multi-grade grouping on student achievement. In this study, sixth-graders performed better when they were taught separately from seventh-graders. Although some sixth-graders performed as well as or better than some seventh-graders when taught in classes that combined the grades, the overall (or average) performance of sixth-graders was not as good as the overall performance of seventh-graders. When I taught sixth-graders separately from seventh-graders, I was able to adjust the lessons to fit their cognitive level. This finding suggests that a year of physical and cognitive maturation, as well as previous school experiences (in this case, in the LMC), may account for improved performance. Multigrade grouping may hinder academic achievement.

Other findings not specifically related to the questions asked of this study include:

- Telephone books are very effective tools for introducing information access skills and concepts to young adolescents. They are free and provide each student with immediate, hands-on experience with a database. The telephone book can be used subsequently throughout the instruction as a paradigm for explaining how electronic databases and indexes work. The skills students learn in using a telephone book are directly transferable to the computer.

- Skills instruction should be broken into concrete steps and each step modeled by the teacher. Review and reinforcement of skills and concepts should be built into the instruction.

Conclusion

As a result of this study, I have a clearer picture of how students learn electronic information access skills and how I can improve my instruction in the library. I have made specific recommendations to my principal and the teaching staff at Sherman for how library skills should be taught next year based on my findings. Before discussing those recommendations, a caveat is in order.

This study was exploratory. I had no control group that I could use for purposes of comparison; instead, I used previous years' instructional programs and the various groups that I taught this year. Furthermore, the results of the posttest and the evaluations may hold no statistical significance. However, all the teachers who participated in this program were pleased with the progress of the students, and we observed carry-over of skills throughout the school year.

Recommendations

I have recommended to the Sherman staff that all sixth-grade students receive formal instruction in electronic information and other library media skills during the 1995–1996 school year. This instruction should be administered to the sixth-graders separately from the seventh-graders. Our principal is encouraging all teachers to schedule LMC instruction for sixth-graders at the outset of the school year.

Since this instruction has not been mandated, and I wish to keep the scheduling of the LMC as flexible as possible, I have proposed another method of reaching all the sixth-graders. Our computer teacher (a former English teacher, as am I) has agreed to team with me to teach research skills during the sixth-grade computer instruction time. All sixth-graders are scheduled into two computer class periods every week for the entire school year. The computer teacher and I will split those classes and teach computer skills and electronic information access skills as part of a larger program in language arts and research skills.

Thanks to this teaming arrangement, I will no longer have to "borrow" students or rely on the cooperation of many other teachers to ensure that sixth-graders receive library skills instruction. While I am working with these students, I will be able to keep the LMC open for use by other students and classes and remain reasonably flexible in my ability to team with other teachers in addition to the computer teacher. I will also have the time and the means to address the development of language arts skills that will help low achievers become effective library users. And I will also embark on another action research study to determine the value of this new format for employing the skills program that I implemented and examined this school year.

Chapter Eight

Building Technological Expertise Among Teachers

Esther Bobowick

What are the unique demands made on staff
development by technology? A view on these
demands is provided by a teacher, library media
specialist, principal, and staff developer.

The advent of information technology in schools presents a unique
set of problems for the professional development of teachers. The
use of technology in schools requires continual professional development to acquaint users with new software, new hardware, and
how to effectively integrate technology into curriculum, instruction, and assessment. Further, technology requires just-in-time support to deal with hardware and software problems. It has become
clear that the successful implementation of technology requires a
vision of what staff development and technical support are needed
and the commitment to revisit what has and has not worked.
Schools are beginning to think about staff development in new
ways. There needs to be an alignment between a staff development
event (such as a workshop or institute) and the need for ongoing
learning and support during implementation of new strategies in
the classroom.

This poses an uncertainty that is wrought by a number of factors. The first factor is the ongoing experimentation with technology in the classroom. Stable practices are not clearly identified as
of yet and therefore best practices cannot be promulgated.

Second, the type of instruction associated with technology promotes more self-directed and group learning from students. These are largely less structured events that require a shift in the traditional design of the classroom and the role of the teacher. Students are now required to share computers and plan together to distribute tasks and resources. Teachers balance their instruction between creating a scaffold for knowledge through direct instruction and coaching students as they gather and construct knowledge through accessing a wide range of resources.

Third, the difference in knowledge between students and teachers is often blurred. Students may educate teachers on the use of the hardware and software. This is certainly a new form of staff development. The culture of computers presents the image of a culture of *help*—help desks, help lines, and technical help. Teachers, who often pride themselves on independence in the classroom, must now become comfortable with asking for help.

Finally, teachers are faced with the logic of a machine and have to spend time learning how to use it to some reasonable degree. "Techno-anxiety" is common, as teachers are afraid of "breaking" the machines or ruining software, or are bewildered by the quirkiness of technology.

These sundry conditions challenge the staff developer to invent new ways to support the much needed human resources for success with technology.

The Gap Between Technology and Human Resource Capabilities

Given these types of challenges to the development of human resources, it is no surprise that technology is often not strongly adopted. The report by Market Data Retrieval, "Technology in Education 1998," takes a comprehensive look at technology use in the nation's K–12 public schools. The data show the following:

1. Although 23 percent of schools report that virtually all of their teachers use computers daily, almost 22 percent report

that none of their teachers use computers daily for instructional purposes.

2. Only 7 percent of schools report that the majority of their teachers are at an advanced skill level (able to integrate technology use into the curriculum). Nearly 38 percent of the schools classified the majority of their teachers as beginners (learning basics), and 43 percent are at intermediate skill level (use a variety of applications).

3. Internet access has increased dramatically: 85 percent of schools now have Internet access, and 44 percent of all classrooms have Internet access.

These results also tell us that schools are rolling out the hardware and the access, but staff are not prepared to utilize these resources fully. To close the gap we must provide educators with quality learning experiences based on our knowledge about how adults learn, and provide continuing support that promotes opportunities for reflection, coaching, modeling, and self-assessment.

Establishing the Dialogue

We should acknowledge that the administrator plays a key role in initiating a process that allows staff to examine and question what the school is trying to accomplish and how it will succeed in doing so. A sequence of dialogues with staff would illuminate specific needs for continuous development that are grounded in both vision and reality.

Collaboration can be modeled by the administrator by posing a series of questions for staff to explore, for example:

- What will students know and be able to do as a result of having been here for X number of years?
- How do we use our current collective expertise to accomplish this?
- Where are the gaps between what we collectively know and need to know that would increase our ability to lead students to these outcomes and beyond?

- How can we acquire the resources that would allow us to sustain the acquisition and implementation of the knowledge over time and thereby better study the impact and effects of such knowledge on student learning?

These dialogues help staff identify areas of development, what they know, and what they need to know to direct their learning. Interested staff can become involved in knowledge building and can support one another through the struggle of organizational learning. Most significantly, dialogue builds an atmosphere of shared learning—one in which the power of knowledge is distributed. The administrator joins the community as a colearner. The staff take responsibility for setting their own learning agenda.

Staff development is no longer the answer to a question that has not been asked. Rather, the inquiry into the uses of technology becomes a significant question for all members of the organization.

New questions arise as we close the gap between our human resources and how they are presently involved with learning and how they become a part of a continuously learning organization. Our models for staff development are presently designed as discrete, credit-bearing events. With the introduction of technology, we define learning as life-long in a rapidly changing environment. The implications for such learning are as follows:

Technology learning requires far more hands-on experiences. Hands-on experiences require new ways of thinking. For example, when you first start to use the word processor, you might think that you are simply replacing your electric typewriter. But as you become a bit more proficient with word processing, you realize that it changes the way you think about writing. Editing is an entirely different process. Previously, you might have more of the editorial function embedded in your writing, leaving your writing less fluent and original. Now, with the word processor, you find that you allow more thoughts to flow onto the screen, realizing that editing is as simple as highlight and delete! So to suggest that learning to use the computer must be hands-on is too limited. It also requires the learner to be placed in authentic experiences that show the skills in relation to the new ways of thinking.

Learners are constantly experiencing cognitive dissonance. The learners' paradigm has not shifted, it is shifting. Learning facilitators need to have the skills to bring the learners through these dissonant times without rescuing them from learning. In other words, skilled facilitators know how to appreciate the fact that whoever's hand is on the mouse is the learner and that the learner needs to have the opportunity to be metacognitive about their learning. They must be able to stand back from the experience *(meta)* and translate it into language *(cognitive)*.

Schools must become clearer about what kind of data they want, how they intend to use it, and how they can structure what they know in order to make the best use of the information. For example, teachers must have clarity about the design of student-centered curriculum units. They need to be able to describe what it is that the students need to know, and be able to do, as a result of the unit of study. They need to be able to design an assessment measure that will tell them what the students have learned. In terms of the use of technology, the unit design will need to be formatted in such a way that other teachers can gain access to the production of such knowledge. This implies agreements about format, what is important in that course of study and how it will be named, and assessment data and how they can be made comparable across grade levels. The significant dialogues in a school are now about knowledge creation and how to retrieve, analyze, and use information about student progress.

Using Diverse Staff Knowledge
to Build Human Resources

In the following case study, we can examine more closely how this works at the school level. A team of teachers from an elementary school in Fairfield, Connecticut, were involved in a one-week summer staff development institute. The institute is designed to have participants build a multimedia, interdisciplinary project that will be evaluated on the last day. This design encompasses the following learning components:

- Working in teams
- Designing an interdisciplinary unit
- Learning to use the technology required for a multimedia presentation
- Working in a learning environment in which the teachers are coaches
- Working with students as teachers
- Learning how to evaluate a multimedia project through teams' evaluation of their own projects
- Considering the implications of how to bring this back to their school
- Reviewing their technology plans after working for a week in a technology-integrated classroom

In what follows, the key members of the Fairfield team reflect on their learning.

Team Perspectives: Teacher, Fifth Grade, Deanna Culbert

I am an active participant in the transformation of professional development in our school. Not too long ago teachers were herded into an auditorium on a staff release day or afternoon to be "inspired" by a single speaker. Often the theme was a blanket message that spanned the K–12 gamut. Some workshops had little relevance to what was actually taking place in the classroom. The impact of this type of professional development lasted a few days or a week at the most, and then we went back to business as usual. Over the years, professional development for teachers has become more pertinent and personal. This changing process is allowing me to become an active, continuous learner alongside my students.

At Cooperative Educational Services I participated in a five-day immersion workshop, the Institute for Information Age Education. Throughout the sessions, I was constantly asking myself, How am I going to use these techniques with my students? As a participant I took on the role of a pupil using technology. In the workshop, learning styles were identified and became the seeds for generating diversified group productivity. I was required to deal with individuals in a situation in which the strengths and weaknesses of all team members, including mine, became pronounced.

We orchestrated an approach to learning whereby one person from each group attended a clinic (miniworkshop) to learn how to perfect a particular skill, such as scanning or using the digital camera. The "expert" then returned to the original group to explain the newly acquired skill. At the end of each day we reflected on our progress and set goals for the following session. The culmination of the weeklong workshop was a day of sharing our final projects. The learning didn't end when the five days were over. Follow-up was extensive, as we were encouraged to share frustrations, successes, and individual accomplishments with the technology projects we were directing back in our classrooms. Specific time was delegated for this important focus. A year later, we are still analyzing and learning through meetings and questionnaires.

Personally, I am now using similar small group formulas in my classroom. Students are often selected to work together according to their learning styles. They create essential questions, set goals for themselves, and reflect on those goals daily. They produce an ongoing time line that keeps team members on a self-imposed schedule. They create a final-product rubric that is instrumental in the self-assessment process. Specialized clinics are held for one student to learn a technique to be brought back to the others. I have two roving troubleshooting "experts" (students) who are always on call to solve technology problems. My students are self-directed learners; they follow the practices I experienced personally in the Institute.

Setting personal goals for the year is a critical part of my professional development. What is new about this procedure is that various staff members are always available to help me accomplish them. At my school, collaboration is a priority, and I would not hesitate to turn to other professionals for guidance. For example, I have taken advantage of our technology rover professional development strand when a substitute came to my classroom and our library media specialist gave me one-on-one instruction to create a Web page. The format for this page was classroom generated, and it was most valuable to have immediate follow-up with my students.

What impresses me most is that curriculum is driving my professional development, and this makes my experience pertinent and exciting. I have spent valuable professional development time creating and working on a flexible schedule that is mine alone. I also participated in a Microsoft PowerPoint clinic at my school. One teacher from each grade level attended and took back the knowledge learned to his or her grade-level colleagues. I gained more from teaching this skill to others than I did acquiring it for myself; the end result is that I feel accomplished in this area.

It was a humbling eye-opener for me to find my technology skill level on a schoolwide rubric. Here I was, stuck in the middle skill level when I thought I knew so much! The questions came quick and fast. How much did I really know? What did I need to have in my repertoire of skills? Was I ready to share the information I knew well? What was it going to take to get me from point D to point H in my learning? How does technology best fit into my ready-made curriculum? Continuous self-evaluation is critical to my growth as a teacher, and it is an essential and effective part of my professional development.

My administrator enthusiastically promotes teacher growth outside the confines of our school district. I look forward to an Internet seminar in New York City. Professional development monies will pay for me, the library media specialist, and my fifth-grade colleagues to attend this all-day intensive session. My curiosity led me to choose this workshop. Based on other seminars I have attended I know my personal technology goal will be stretched and satisfied. I look forward to bringing back new skills, ideas, and enthusiasm to my classroom.

I think of myself as a continuous, active learner alongside my students. Professional development, if done effectively, takes me as I am and moves me along a constantly adjusted continuum of guided self-growth. I want to be inspired to invent—to take what is there and specialize it for my fifth graders. I want to be open to ideas and experimentation without limits. I want to take the unexpected and twist it to my own satisfaction. I want to create a world of surprises with my pupils so that we all feel exhilarated. Technology training through professional development is my infrastructure, well grounded in information age educational philosophy. I see it as my beginning—an opportunity to change the way my students and I view the world.

Team Perspectives: The Library Media Specialist, Dorna Perrson

The elementary school introduction to Fairfield's districtwide library media curriculum for information literacy and technology skills states, "Children at the elementary school level possess intellectual curiosity and confidence in their ability to use technology to answer questions, solve problems, and communicate solutions." We, as teachers and library media specialists, must gain the same confidence in our ability to facilitate our students' answering questions, solving problems, and communicating solutions through technology. Empowering teachers with these skills presents an enormous challenge to a school. The school library media specialist, as a curriculum specialist, instructional leader, and person responsible for the implementation of technology, is afforded a unique perspective on the needs of staff with regard to technology. Each teacher's response to technology and to the changes it requires in curriculum delivery is unique, thus requiring a multi-faceted approach to professional development.

Recognizing this challenge, the library media and technology advisory committee mapped a plan for technology professional development. We began with looking at what skills were needed to meet teacher, and ultimately student, needs. After studying several technology rubrics from various sources, we created a technology rubric for our teachers. Teachers placed themselves on the rubric, and we compiled the information we gleaned from these rubrics in graph form. As expected, teachers were at different levels of expertise over a range of technology skills. By combining the information depicted on the graphs with the knowledge of the many different levels of comfort and stress our teachers associated with technology, we gained a good picture of where we stood and where we needed to build our skills.

Our next step was to brainstorm, *How?* Several good ideas were offered, and we realized that each of these ideas met a specific need. Why not offer a multifaceted approach? The resulting plan offered technology professional development opportunities, or strands, to meet each teacher where she or he was in terms of technology knowledge and provide appropriate support for each one's growth. The opportunities included clinics, "critical friends for technology integration," coaches for self-directed learners, technology "rover" days, large group overviews, and small-group, just-in-time workshops.

To date, this year at our school, *clinics* have been offered in the use of the digital camera, PowerPoint, and Inspiration software. The design of these clinics, learned at the Institute for Information Age Education, leads to powerful professional development at several levels. One teacher from each grade level, as well as specialists, can attend each clinic, thus resulting in a small group of learners, which is ideal for hands-on learning. Each teacher in attendance must agree to teach the clinic content to the rest of her or his grade-level teachers. This results in many teachers taking responsibility for technology professional development and in deeper learning for the original clinic participants. A large number of teachers have been trained, yet the training has occurred in small groups with little time spent by any one trainer. Each participant is required to write about classroom applications for the technology learned, and we are compiling technology integration booklets for the staff.

The most challenging area for technology professional development is the integration of technology into the curriculum. We have designed the *critical friends for technology integration* strand to meet this need. Each teacher who would like help in discovering creative ways to improve student learning through the use of technology can ask for another teacher to help her or him over the course of the school year. This critical friend might observe in the teacher's classroom, identifying times when technology could be introduced, brainstorm ideas with the teacher, or simply listen to the teacher's concerns and offer specific feedback. When speaking of her critical friend, one teacher reflected that her guidance helped her both organize her integration ideas and gain new ones.

In our *self-directed technology learner* strand, a teacher requests another teacher to act as her or his coach for a specific software program or application. Teachers fill out a form at the beginning of the school year, either requesting a coach or volunteering their services as a coach and listing which software applications and programs with which they feel confident enough to help another teacher learn. Teachers are matched with an appropriate coach. Each teacher then proceeds in a self-directed manner to learn the software, knowing that when it is necessary to receive help, his or her coach is there. One teacher stated in our mid-year evaluation of the self-directed learner strand, "The best part was that I was able to see my coach when I needed her and ask my specific questions."

Six teachers have taken advantage of one-to-one instruction on the two *technology "rover"* professional development days we have held so far this year. On these designated days, teachers sign up to meet individually with the library media specialist to receive help in any area of technology they desire. The "rover" is actually the substitute hired to go from classroom to classroom to release teachers for this professional development. Teachers have worked on software ranging from Kid Pix, learning to use stamps for a math lesson, to Claris Home Page, creating a classroom home page for the Internet.

Whole staff overviews serve to introduce staff to possibilities for further exploration. We have offered this year whole-group introduction to PowerPoint and Inspiration with follow-up hands-on clinics. Other overviews this year will include Web site evaluation, Web searching techniques, and an overview of Web sites helpful to teachers.

Just-in-time small group workshops are held during a grade-level common planning time and offer review or new learning to a grade-level team of teachers just before their students need to use a particular piece of software or application. One such workshop was held for our fourth-grade teachers prior to their students setting up a spreadsheet to record daily weather as part of a science unit.

In addition to these strands, our teachers attend districtwide technology workshops, as well as ones offered by outside consultants. The follow-up opportunities to these learning experiences that are built into our multifaceted, school-based design increase the chances that teachers will be able to exploit the new learning.

Team Perspectives: The Principal, Gary Kass

When I think about what I do that motivates staff to change, I would have to say I simply ask them what they want to learn and what support they will need to do so. The traditional teacher evaluation system is often perceived as one sided—that I, as the principal, am only interested in evaluating what they have done so far with little or no response to what they hope to become. That is not my interpretation of evaluation. I am interested in continuous growth and learning and I use my role as evaluator to encourage and support new learning as much as to observe what is already learned.

Educators as Continuous Learners

In the beginning of the school year we have faculty meetings to talk about what schoolwide goals we want to set and what individual learning goals we want to achieve through professional development within the year. The results are fodder for the professional development team as they use the agreed-upon schoolwide and individual goals as the basis for the school professional development plan.

I see my staff as lifelong learners and I take responsibility for facilitating that learning on a very personal level. I meet with teachers informally and ask: What are you working on? What do you want to be when you grow up? In individual conversations, I learn where the fear or resistance to change comes from. For some it's lack of confidence; for others it's lack of resources or an understanding of where to begin to find the resources. For still others it's a lack of belief that anyone really cares what they think.

Finding out what they want to learn and helping them get there provides evidence for the staff that I am serious about wanting to support teachers in their journey. I also am willing to share where my individual goals lie and what I am trying to do to fulfill my part of the schoolwide goals.

Many principals are afraid to show their ignorance with technology. They need to be humble enough to say, "Hey I need to learn how to use all these new tools, too!" and participate in training alongside their staff. If a principal can help teachers meet their individual goals, the excitement comes through in their teaching. The students get very enthusiastic about the work when they see the passion the teachers bring to the instruction. This has been particularly true with technology. Teachers who have gravitated toward technology, had training, and used the tools have quickly identified ways to integrate technology into their curriculum. Others, who may be reluctant to use it and have not been supported in their journey to learn about it, send a clear message to their students that this is something we will deal with later, . . . much later.

Maintenance

I have found three actions to be of help in supporting teachers as they try to meet the goals we set regarding technology:

1. Meeting with grade-level teams during common planning time on a regular basis and listening while they talk about what they are working on and what they need in order to be successful.

2. Letting staff know I am excited about my own learning as I try to meet my individual goals. For example, I talk with enthusiasm about the upcoming PowerPoint workshop that I will attend because it encompasses one of my personal goals.

3. Demonstrating support by providing for time with staff through ten monthly faculty meetings in which the focus is on professional development (the announcements are handled through written correspondence).

The Biggest Challenge

The biggest challenge I face as I work with my staff is to make certain that I do not overwhelm them with everything they need to do and know. Knowing how to be an effective motivator and gatekeeper requires a great deal of "situational leadership"—trying to keep everyone working at the pace at which they are most effective and are still learning.

The second biggest challenge is the integration of new staff. How do I bring on people who share this vision of collaboration? Maintaining a balance of engaging people and doing business is the tension of administration. As we face the challenge of technology, that balance becomes an even greater concern. I have based my practice on the assumption that in order for faculty to become more technologically literate and be able to bring technology meaningfully to the students, they will have to work collaboratively. The people component of collaboration takes time and care. At the same time, we are always overwhelmed by a task component. How can we cover all the standards, prepare our students for the statewide tests, introduce new people on staff to the collaborative process, and continue our learning growth as a faculty? We juggle time as we make this a priority. The payoff has been wonderful.

Team Perspectives: The Staff Developer, Esther Bobowick

After the teachers attended the weeklong professional development Institute, I provided on-site technical assistance back at their school in order to support the application of their new knowledge. We always start with the school's instructional priorities (for example, their new science curriculum, writing literacy, performance assessments). In working with the interdisciplinary fifth-grade team, we engaged in the following process:

- What are the desired outcomes? We identified the results they wanted from their students and the strategies they wanted to use to get there.
- How does technology fit? We looked at the possible applications of technology that would lead students to those results.
- Do we have the resources and capabilities? To address this question, we talked about the availability of the resources and expertise among the staff to provide them. Where we found the expertise was absent (for example, for creating a Web site), we identified how staff might acquire those skills.
- How will we measure success? We looked for "indicators of success" for students. For example, using technology with the curriculum can provide teachers with rich observations about how their students approach new learning and use previous knowledge.

We can see what true student engagement looks like as we observe students involved in authentic projects, such as using computers to access information, creating presentations, and developing teams. We can measure productivity based on the amount of time they spend on the task and the quality of the work they produce as a result of having access to a richer array of resources. We can observe what habits of mind, attitudes, and dispositions students need to develop in order to apply their knowledge and skills.

We set up a series of meetings and expectations for work to be done in my absence. Such meetings focused on the use of technology in the curriculum, how teachers design lessons and units in conjunction with technology, and where they can test their understanding of the use of technology. When the group reconvened, they examined student work and discussed the quality of the work produced. Did it meet the criteria established? Was there evidence of effective use of technology? What do we know about the level of student understanding about the content of the work presented?

At the end of the year, I met with the principal, the library media specialist, and the teachers to establish benchmarks for change as we looked to next year. We discussed the problems we were having and attended to feedback so that we could continuously realign our goals with desired and current student outcomes. This feedback spiral was used to look ahead and inform the school of their accomplishments.

Conclusion

The feedback spiral guided the professional development process at the Fairfield, Connecticut, elementary school. We began with defining our purposes and worked our way out to planning and implementation. From the perspective of the team, we can see the power of a new staff development model. This particular case study shows how we addressed the critical challenges raised in the beginning of this chapter. We were able to create a learning environment that was empowering for the staff. Teachers became knowledge workers—constructing new unit designs, learning about their work with students as they attended to their own learning, and taking the time to analyze and reflect on their learning so that it can be documented.

The implementation of the feedback spiral and the cultivation of knowledge workers emerged from four conditions:

1. Recognizing the need to learn
2. Identifying the benefits for students from new learning

3. Building an environment of trust so that personnel are willing to take the inherent risk of new learning

4. Knowing that resources and support are available

Establishing these four conditions requires a commitment on the part of leadership to this kind of learning, guided by an attractive vision of what the investment in learning will create. Without the resources and the vision, the heart and soul of this process will weaken and founder.

Reference

Market Data Retrieval. "Technology in Education 1998." [http://www.school-data.com]. 1998.

Chapter Nine

Creating an Information Infrastructure

Challenges for the Future

Bena Kallick, James M. Wilson III

> Successfully implementing an information system
> aimed at improving student performance faces a
> number of challenges.

As they enter the twenty-first century, schools are attempting to implement a systems view of continuous growth and improvement through a careful analysis of information about student learning. This movement is driven by the demand for knowledge about the causes and effects of student performance at the state, district, building, classroom, and student levels. The information-processing power of technology makes this goal much more viable than it has been in the past.

The signs of this increasing demand for knowledge are evident in school conversations that have shifted in focus from objectives to student outcomes. Data about student learning are becoming organized through curriculum mapping, assessment data are more systematically documented, and local, state, and national standards are being developed as benchmarks for learning. A new level of understanding about teaching and learning is emerging.

Emerging development of electronic information systems to support this demand for information and knowledge is in the formative stage. Many experiments are in progress. The technological power stands ready to be employed, but the creation of the information systems that truly support understanding is lagging. To use knowledge as a resource, schools need a method for structuring information, promoting and preserving organizational learning, and developing the staff as "knowledge workers" so that knowledge is both used and continues to be created.

Creating knowledge requires a method, as noted in Chapter One. The *feedback spiral* guides the method of knowledge creation. It suggests that learning and innovation should move through a series of steps that will ultimately provide the basis for decisions about continuation and improvement of actions that seek to enhance student performance. When a group uses the feedback spiral, it details the cycle of learning and, what is most important, asks itself to return to its original purposes and review its intention and direction. This process reminds a group to determine whether its original purposes have been well served in the initial round of implementation and to address questions uncovered in the process of implementation and change. In returning to goals and outcomes, the group might find that their experimentation took them further from rather than closer to their desired ends. Yet the group may see the next steps for furthering the work based on their data analysis.

The feedback spiral promotes knowledge work that is guided by data rather than impressions. A key learning for organizations is that data from the *process* are as significant as data from the *outcomes*. As we consider the challenges to implementing a system guided by the feedback spiral, we must deal with the vestiges of how work was conducted before the prospect of continuous learning based on the use of information technology existed. Other challenges arise out of the technology itself and the nature of how we collect and make sense of data and information.

An organization that attempts to use the feedback spiral to create knowledge must confront a number of technical, cultural, and human resource challenges to implement an information system successfully that can develop the knowledge aimed at improving student performance. We examine eight challenges to the successful implementation of such an information system.

Challenge One: Increased Service

Today we are challenged by standards-driven assessments that require rethinking curriculum, instruction, and assessment. Such changes have emerged from a world driven by information technology and customer service. For example, only ten years ago, when a car was taken to the garage for its thirty-thousand-mile check-up, it was possible that you would be told the unfortunate news that it was a "lemon." Now you are more likely to have a range of quality checks regarding your satisfaction with the performance of the car: a follow-up phone call after service was provided, a survey for degree of satisfaction, a reminder of when the next service is required, perhaps even a "report card" for you to fill out. We are told that even the IRS is concerned with service!

Likewise, in education we now talk about our "customers" or "stakeholders." We are learning how to focus on service and what the community can recognize as quality. To this end, we also provide surveys and more frequent communication and reporting systems. Schools are working feverishly to become more dynamic and responsive to this need for service. To increase the quality of a service means knowing more about what we are doing and also informing "customers" about what is known. Hence, we are beginning to realize the need to build information systems in schools that serve the purpose of improving our practice as educators so as to improve student performance, and also to inform stakeholders of those very efforts to improve student performance.

Although every school system has information about student performance, when the time comes to make important decisions about students, we often have to track down information from a variety of places (see Chapter Three). In addition, we often do not have sufficient information to make decisions about courses of study, appropriate interventions, curriculum changes, and instructional decisions—all of which greatly affect the learner's performance. Some data are in spreadsheets, some on "hard-copy" in manila folders, some on the district's mainframe, some on a Macintosh computer, others on a PC. Schools are beginning to realize that information technology can make it possible, for the first time, to organize these disparate pieces so that they are available for making decisions and creating reports.

The movement toward organizationwide data systems, accessible to all stakeholders, is gaining steam. The new buzz-words you have heard or are likely to hear are about data-warehousing, data marts, decision support systems, middleware, drill-down, data mining, and OLAP (on-line analytical processing). These all point to integrating organizational data and making it amenable to answering any question posed to the organization. Answering such questions from within or from stakeholders outside the organization will improve service as each question helps focus and refocus our knowledge about the concerns of educators and the public with regard to student performance.

Challenge Two: Changing the Culture

Effective problem solving will require collaboration. At the system level, teams of teachers will need to exchange their insights and learning. This requires new learning—a new set of habits for communication and collaboration. There is a far greater individual will for teaching than a collective will to work together as a team. Although some exchange takes place within a department or at a grade level, usually only limited exchange occurs across levels or buildings within a district. Teamwork is usually defined as "another committee," and the work of the committee is usually more laborious than knowledge building. The mode of one classroom at a time, one teacher at a time, will need to shift to the whole school community, in teams, taking responsibility for student learning over time. Schools rarely time for analysis of data; when the data are brought forward, they are usually in such a reduced form that learning about individual students is lost.

The conversations about what is important for students to know and be able to do, for example, are now a public and explicit conversation. The reason the discussions have become more public is that in order to make sense out of curriculum, instruction, and assessment, we now see the potential of documenting our work in electronic form. As we move toward doing so, our thinking becomes available to all teachers in the organization, not just the grade level or the building. With such availability of information, new teachers, when they enter the district, will have access to the thinking of teachers from across the district.

Since our first point is the need for clarity, we are taking the time to become more precise about what transpires in classrooms (see, for example, Jacobs, 1997). However, developing the maps and coming to agreements and understandings requires collaboration. Discussions about curriculum, instruction, and assessment have brought forward two strong psychological states:

- We are finally talking about what is important and can see some continuity to our work.
- We are concerned that all of these discussions will take away our individuality and creativity.

We will be pressed to be more uniform about everything that we do. Each of these states of mind is real and alive for teachers who have been through such discussions many times. Teachers are concerned about whether this information will, in fact, benefit what they care most about: making certain that all students are learning in their classrooms.

With the advent of information technology, we now have greatly refined methods for studying the cause-and-effect relationships between what goes on in the classroom and measurements of learning. It will take experience to build confidence in the possibilities that this work portends. For example, with the use of a spreadsheet, data can be constructed. Once constructed, a variety of graphing strategies can be employed to show correlations and multidimensional relationships within and across data.

Knowledge creation thrives on a variety of information. Comparing, contrasting, and correlating information from various sources in an organization provide a reality check. Considerable richness in the diversity of perspectives makes such knowledge more likely to be valid and useful.

Information technology has opened the possibility of sharing among teachers as they build knowledge from their common experiences. However, as schools are presently designed, addressing the following issues becomes a challenge:

- Talking about students as though they are shared by all teachers and through many years, rather than considering each year as "my classroom," "my kids"

- Thinking of curriculum as a continuous story of learning in which last year's work rests on the shoulders of this year's work, with an ongoing feedback system about what is actually accomplished year by year, given the differences in the chemistry of classes and additional demands that are not predictable

- Determining what best practices bring about the most likely conditions for student improvement and documenting what works so that teachers can learn from one another without attending many meetings

- Sharing all of this with one another in a formal way based on the evidence of student work as well as the evidence of grades and teacher impressions

Hence, implementing a system that provides information useful to instruction and assessment must begin with some very elemental questions about what information matters, how much can be usefully shared, and what the incentives are for teachers to share innovations in instruction with their colleagues. The challenge to the culture is to create a safe and trusting environment in which teachers feel protected from the evaluation of administrators and their colleagues so that they can build new knowledge about student learning. Since the culture does not, at this time, encourage such work, educators depend on academic researchers to provide the knowledge. Although the development of external knowledge is significant, it must interact with the internal knowledge of the teachers within the system. Otherwise, there will continue to be suspicion, rejection, or swings to practices that may not fit the vision and goals of the school district.

Challenge Three: Deciding What Information Should Be Collected and Who Decides

Who decides what information to collect? Understanding what information matters requires asking questions among the members of the organization, as well as drawing on the expertise of consultants versed in educational research and knowledge. In understanding the questions and needs of practitioners one begins to create the knowledge base of the organization and to delineate the baseline for indicators and measures for significant change.

It is important to build consensus about what matters in terms of information, for without consensus there may not be adoption of a system that employs such information. If the users of the information system are not asked about what matters, you may find that they deem what you create useless. The key is uncovering this "practical knowledge." Without the focus on the "practical," the system will not be used. The organization will fragment into dozens of experiments, as teachers will create their own systems for making sense of their work and enact their own feedback spiral "in exile." Again, this points to the very social aspect of information use. You want to create a learning community, so you need to start with a community from the very start to build the information infrastructure.

The "sharing" of information and notions of what matters is critical to the success of creating information systems that provide practical knowledge. For example, currently many schools have little information that serves as a longitudinal record of what curriculum students have engaged with, classroom by classroom; what instructional strategies have been attempted to meet the needs of students, individually; and what assessment data have been used to determine whether students are learning. In the very place where the objective—improving student performance through instruction— is determined, the organization of data, information, and knowledge is often the weakest. The knowledge in this area is tacit and idiosyncratic because the management of student learning has historically been decentralized at the classroom level.

When we take a student-centered approach and consider the problems students may have with so much variety in teaching and expectations of learning, we begin to realize that we must formalize the exchange among teachers regarding these matters. This does not mean that we need to create more uniform practices in the classroom. It does mean that we need to come to a consensus about our interpretation of standards, common scoring practices through the use of rubrics, and curriculum mapping to determine what is being taught when, and what kind of expectations members of the organization can share.

Challenge Four: Creating Shared Categories of Information to Build the Information Infrastructure

Creating a useful information system requires a clear articulation of names of things and their relationships. For example, when we have multiple rubrics to score writing, multiple criteria for what constitutes quality, and different information collected about student writing from year to year, it is difficult to build systematic information about students that might help us understand the effectiveness of program, curriculum, assessments, and the degree of improvement in student learning. We already have, in print, too many file folders that are moved from one year to the next without a clear articulation of purpose and organization for comparability. When matters are not made clear, you experience GIGO: garbage in, garbage out. It is this exactness that at times drives humans, not machines, "buggy." However, moving to a greater level of clarity is part of the continuous journey of learning.

To make the best use of technology we must make the inarticulate, articulate; the fuzzy, sharp.

The information that will be used will be stored in databases. Database software used in an organization requires that there be a *common set of categories of information*. This set of categories defines what information can be stored and retrieved easily. For example, when considering a computerized student record, there must be a decision made as to what sets of information will comprise that record. This means the organization must make choices as to what matters in terms of knowing about a student: What does the information indicate to us about student performance? What data can be collected in a reliable fashion about the student? How are those data stored over time and made retrievable?

Well-structured data make it possible to analyze information at the district level over years, teachers, subjects, school buildings, race and ethnicity, gender, and grade, to name a few. If the data structure is well designed—that is, developed through a process of inquiry that examines the real value of every piece of data collected—then the organization can use this information to manage the content and processes in delivering education to students. Such information, gathered over time, begins to develop a set of indicators about the performance of the district, buildings, classes, and students.

When a district is guided by a set of indicators for performance and appropriate developmental benchmarks of progress, they can establish a feedback system (see Chapter One) to guide their inquiry and decisions. In our current state, there is not an agreed upon set of indicators. There are many possibilities that can give educators an understanding of what influences student performance. For example:

- How is attendance correlated with grades?
- How is the time of day a class is held correlated with grades?
- Do new teachers grade differently from older teachers?
- How different are the achievement scores in each class?

- What is the frequency of disciplinary actions and how does that correlate with classrooms students are referred from?
- What are the reading aptitude scores of students, and how does that predict outcomes in other knowledge domains?
- What is considered reasonable progress for students from particular socioeconomic backgrounds? What sort of progress has there been historically?

Many more questions can develop indicators, and it is important for an organization to know what its questions are. Discussing and answering these questions is how learning takes place, and recording the conclusions and observing the results of actions taken on the basis of this information is how knowledge is created. In other words, these questions are what drives knowledge creation.

Ignoring questions makes an organization unresponsive and seemingly irrational to its members. However, to build the capability to answer questions requires creating an information infrastructure to support answering questions, and a dedication to keeping such information up to date. If the process breaks down, the information will not be timely or accurate and faith in the process will erode.

The set of questions in a school begins to suggest how the data should be organized and what demands should be put on the information technology to allow you to answer such questions.

Recognize that creating shared categories to describe curriculum, instructional methods, and assessments is a double-edged sword. You want to create an information system that has consensus among organizational members, is in line with organizational objectives, and has been generated by the organizational questions. Yet given that curriculum, instruction, and assessment are evolving with learning, the process of *reconfiguring* information will be ongoing. The information system needs to have the capability to handle new categories that emerge through greater understanding and through innovation by the organization. The information system must be allowed to change or it will become obsolete—the task of maintaining its stability used to suppress organizational innovation.

Practically speaking, information structure should reign for a particular cycle——say one to two years. Ideas about improving the system should be gathered for its revision. Hence, schools may be seen to adopt the "version" strategy of software vendors. As with software, schools must live with their information paradigm until the next cycle replaces the existing version. This process allows periods of stability, albeit imperfect, to exist while you are institutionalizing change in the information system by being attentive to suggestions and complaints that guide design for the next cycle. Without creating formal cycles of change, the information system will never be stable. We do not suggest "thriving on chaos" in this case.

Also note that change in the information has potential costs, beyond just the financial. Such changes disrupt the time series of data. Each innovation that changes the structure of the database often makes the new data incommensurable to some degree with the old. They are different data, and therefore the history of the organization, captured with certain information, may be quite erratic. For example, if you change the scale used on your assessments every year, you lose the longitudinal record unless you are willing to rescale everything you collected in the past.

Challenge Five: Defining Private Versus Public Information

Information within an organization can be broadly divided into public information and private information. For example, a teacher may be entertaining a hypothesis about a student or a concern about her own methods of teaching. This is information that the teacher uses to reflect on student evaluation and self-evaluation. It is for her process of understanding, and it best remains private so that such nascent concepts can develop before being made public. In addition, many teachers feel that the practices they have are specialized to a particular student or their own particular interests. They do not feel that sharing is necessarily advantageous to the group.

However, other information should be public so that the organization, as a whole, can understand what it is doing and if it is meeting its objectives. So student grades, assessment results of various kinds, attendance, and other data that inform how the organization as a whole is moving needs to be in a form that can be easily shared and analyzed. This is the information that will be used to develop the indicators about the status of the district, schools, classes, and students.

There are numerous questions that districts will have to face about access to the district's information. Should parents be able to log into the school network to find out about their child's homework and current grades? If so, then the system administrator needs to have a carefully considered strategy for security. This raises the question as to how much information should be available to the general public. What data are made available needs to be considered among the stakeholders of education in the local community.

The degree of "public-ness" of data also raises the question of competition among teachers. Will such sharing lead to parents comparing the assignments from one teacher to another? Will this increase the number of parental requests for a particular teacher? Will this generate more questions from parents about the nature of work in the classroom? If we believe the research that suggests that parents are a most significant factor in relation to a student's learning, then we must find ways to keep parents more informed. They need to have information about curriculum, instruction, and student progress. The common concerns about parental involvement are highlighted with the possibility of every teacher having a Web page for such communication, or every student a Web page for perusal.

The key point here is that if you are going to make data public, you need to have a strategy for managing the reaction to it. This means focusing on "managing" the demand for information on the district. A district must think through how it will handle the reaction to particular information and the demand for its information. Making all data available is not a public relations panacea. It can be a Pandora's box if the meaning and implications of such data are not fully pondered.

Challenge Six: Building an Enterprisewide Integrated Information System

The agenda of the knowledge-creating organization is to enhance our capability to look at the system as a whole and see the relationship between classrooms and buildings within and across the district. With such information we can observe trends and patterns through statistical as well as qualitative analyses. An electronic information system can take advantage of tools that enhance systems thinking, such as maps and diagrams that show the relationship among multiple aspects of the organization.

Although we have known the need for greater understanding of interdependent relationships in schools, we have been unable to track them sufficiently with tools that depict various forms of interdependence. With information technology we can identify causal loops, use feedback spirals to describe our continuous learning, and look simultaneously at the data from a set of schools within a district and match them to demographic information. In other words, we can think systemically rather than considering each part of the system as though it were unrelated to the whole. Designing an information system that can provide analysis at each level of the organization presents the challenge of thinking through how the data will be gathered and information generated that is of value at each of the levels.

Knowledge is made from the important building blocks of data collection and information analysis. A school needs to be able to analyze what is happening at the student level, classroom level, building level, and district level. At each level the data needed for subsequent levels need to be considered. Otherwise, the information system becomes fragmented and the kind of enterprisewide analysis that is required is disabled.

Student Level

Our studies have shown that the information most teachers want about students is centered on the following questions:

- What are the strengths in performance and what needs work?
- What is known about this student over time?
- What samples of work are available to demonstrate previous performances?
- What are the student's test scores from standardized or state tests and how does that relate to how well the student is doing against the benchmarks and standards?
- How well is the student doing as compared with other students in the class? In the grade? Across the district?
- How does the student evaluate his own performance, and what goals does he feel he is working on?

Classroom Level

Information use and need is centered on classroom variance at this level. Teachers want to know the range of differences in student performance. In addition, they are seeking grouping patterns. They want to know which students would work well together, which students could be organized for specific minilessons, which students should have extra help beyond the classroom. Their concern is whether the students are making progress toward the benchmarks that will be measured in the next state or other testing situation. Although classroom teachers place great value on their own assessments, they are particularly concerned about the more public results of the standardized or state measures. Too often, teachers do not receive sufficient information about the next benchmark. For example, a fifth grade teacher is often in a building in which the last benchmark assessment was in the fourth grade. He or she does not have the requirements or examples of the next benchmark test at the eighth grade and, in fact, is not in the same building. As a result, the teacher cannot continue to track progress toward the next set of achievements that will be publicly measured. Therefore, data that are both retrospective and prospective are essential.

Building Level

Administrators have a larger picture than the classroom teacher. Their concern is oriented toward how all of the classes at the sixth grade, for example, are doing in progressing toward the eighth-grade benchmarks. They are interested in a year-by-year analysis across all grades and a class-by-class analysis of performance. They maintain an overview on the interventions that are offered for students and are concerned about the degree to which the interventions are serving the students. In addition, they use data to determine class placements.

District Level

The central office administration, including the superintendent, are concerned with the performance of all the schools. They try to answer the questions of how well the buildings are doing, how well the system as a whole is doing, and whether the resources offered to the buildings for support of students are well utilized toward improved performance. They are required to report to the state, the board, and ultimately to the staff and community about the progress of the system.

To delineate the needs at each level requires collaboration among the educators in the district and clarity about the use of the information. To accomplish such a meaningful integration requires strong leadership that has clear vision and can manage the careful planning to make this happen. This internal knowledge often benefits greatly from external knowledge in the form of consultants who know how to keep such a process focused, aligned with organizational objectives, and implemented in meaningful stages over time.

Challenge Seven: Cultivating Educators as Knowledge Workers

If teachers are to be the creators and sense makers of information, they will need additional skills. They will have to learn how to analyze information, seek patterns in the data, and collaboratively solve the problems that arise as they make sense of the material at hand. They will have to learn how to think at the system level as well as at the classroom level. Given the skills, they will see their role as knowledge workers.

A *knowledge worker* is a worker who is constantly dealing with new situations, learning from them, and attempting to respond in new and better ways. The chief implication of a shift to knowledge work is that knowledge workers adapt their responses to a given situation instead of carrying out standard operating procedures. They attempt to understand an appropriate response to a situation and then marshal the necessary resources and capabilities to get it done.

Teachers as knowledge workers need to gain expertise in looking at student work for evidence of learning and areas of knowledge that need special attention by examining data on students to understand what else might be done to enhance learning and examining their own practices in terms of effectiveness. Teachers need to share what they have learned with each other for validation and to increase understanding within the organization as a whole. Information technology can enhance this process by providing a means to record information that can be analyzed and easily retrieved for reporting.

The good news is that information technology has given us access to increasingly more data. The difficult part of that news, however, is that in order to study data and, as a social group, give it meaning, we will have to change the values of school culture. The most significant changes are to use diverse information, cultivate an analytic approach to information, and share that information to remove biases and refine our knowledge. In order to do this we will need to

1. *Learn how to share our work* in a deeper and more meaningful way. This means examining a broad range of information about a student and sharing hypotheses about why the student is on a particular course.

2. *We will have to develop "habits of mind"* as school faculties (Costa and Kallick, 2000). In a sense, these "habits" are the basic values of scientific community and are thus designed to create knowledge over time. In schools as we know them presently, these habits are rarely present. Hence, knowledge creation is undermined. Such "habits of the mind" include

   Listening with understanding and empathy. Although we all claim to listen to one another, we often do not experience being understood. All groups will need to learn how to listen attentively, paraphrasing to check for understanding, accepting diverse opinions and suspending judgment, and understanding the other's perspective empathetically.

   Flexibility. Groups will have to learn how to be flexible in their thinking. The first answer may not be the best answer. They will have to learn how to tolerate ambiguity as they seek to understand before reacting with solutions.

   Risk taking. Groups will have to take risks in order to learn. The risks will be educated by the information. Yet the greatest challenge for any group is to be loyal to the experiments of others when the results are uncertain.

   Humility of continuous learning. Groups will have to learn the humility of continuous learning. They will have to seek to learn and experience the humility of being a novice as they learn. They will have to learn how to give and accept feedback as a constructive part of their learning.

3. *We will have to create the time for teachers to exchange information about their work with students.* To engage in the feedback
spiral takes time. This includes time to study student work,
study assessment data, and analyze information. We have previously had an informal process for such sharing. We will
have to learn how to find the time not just for planning but
for analyzing information. Schools must make time for knowledge creation among their staff. We will have to learn the
necessary analytic skills for making sense of the data. We will
have to develop the capacity to shape raw data into workable
patterns. We will have to test innovations through a process
of experimentation that requires hypothesis formation, data
gathering, and methods of evaluating results. The school culture will need to support such experimental inquiry.

Challenge Eight: Managing the Politics for Change to a Knowledge Building Culture

Perhaps our greatest challenge is staying the course at a time when
the political focus is on education. The times serve as a reminder
to the adage: Be careful, or you may get what you wished for. Educators have often felt the need for more attention from the public,
a desire for the public to understand the significance and therefore
the need for support. As we have moved into the information age,
this desire has turned to a politics that has us reeling! We have
"education governors" and "education presidents," many of whom
have a desire for short-term results for what educators know is a
long-term process. The following represent some of the challenges
we face as we anchor our schools in a new methodology for knowledge building and learning:

Internal Versus External Knowledge

Schools have traditionally had some confusion about the source of
knowledge. There is a great respect for the research of academics

and, at the same time, a great skepticism about the usefulness of such knowledge in the classroom. Since classroom practitioners spend most of their working hours in the classroom, there is little time or process for them to build knowledge across the years and disciplines. Although most practitioners believe that their practices serve students, they do not believe that their work is constructed around a philosophy or theory of teaching and learning. Asking teachers to become more explicit about their theories is a challenge to most teaching populations. Schools want to hold on to personal theories and at the same time want to bring about a collective experience within the school. Most often, personal theories collide within the building and seek the support of external research. In many ways, this use of external research allows each teacher to feel a broader affirmation of personal theories and less of a need to come to agreements within the microcosm of their schools.

Since information is now more available, there is also a question of what constitutes knowledge only within the profession and what constitutes knowledge that the broader public should understand. Given the new possibility for increased communication through Web sites and electronic mail, many teachers and administrators need to (1) communicate more frequently and (2) decide what is possible that will be understood without a fear of further politicizing the environment.

Finally, educators are self-protective. There is a strong culture of protection about evaluation and feedback. A fundamental assumption of the profession is that it should be noncompetitive. For example, we do not encourage merit pay, we do not encourage incentives that differentiate on the basis of the quality of the work produced. Rather, we attempt to build an organization that learns together on behalf of our students. However, many of our practices indicate that the workplace is highly competitive in behavior in spite of these policies. For example, when test scores are differentiated so that the administrator has information about which classes performed especially well, it is almost impossible to have a grade-level conversation about that information to understand why a particular class may have outperformed the others. The immediate cultural reaction is that differences are understood in light of student differences, not quality of teaching differences. And when external data such as parental requests for particular teachers emerge consistently, the school does not take this on as a collective problem. Rather, it denies such data or discusses them in the parking lot but not at the faculty meeting.

Since schools are presently designed within the paradoxical tension of competition and cooperation, an information management system seriously challenges this culture.

Who Has the Expertise?

Whereas previously schools were organized with positional power, a knowledge-building culture is based on the importance of ideas. This promotes the possibility of distributed knowledge. We may find that some of our best ideas about teaching come from unexpected places. For example, a custodian in a public school in Michigan took a course on portfolio assessment alongside the teaching staff. Since the course was open to any member in the learning community, he thought that he would take the course and build a portfolio for himself. As he learned about the theory and practice of portfolio assessment, and as he gradually started building his own portfolio, he developed some marvelous ideas about teaching from his own learning. This was a departure for teachers who were accustomed to learning in a far more insular environment. Or look at the secretary, for example, who through the input of data about assessment has a great idea about how to sort and analyze the data differently.

Again, teachers have worked long and hard, with the support of their unions, to show their value as professionals and to receive pay commensurate with their professional knowledge and expertise. The threat of distributing the expertise is real from their perception. The shift that needs to be made in terms of building a shared learning culture, using a feedback spiral for increased performance, means that expertise will be defined in terms of getting the questions right, not just in knowing all the solutions.

Settling the Cross-Platform Question

There is an incredible push and pull between the two platforms available in most schools (Macintosh-Apple versus PC-Windows). Money that is allocated for improvements in technology press schools to choose between the two. Often the question is resolved by consultants, either within or outside of the system, who are loyal to and sell one platform or the other. Settling the question is often tied to questionable gain on the part of the consultant.

In addition, there is a push from the technology side of the system to get more technology—new wiring, new computers, more upgrades. As schools begin to move from the novice to the practitioner stage in degree of use of technology, the way technology is used pushes back on the technocrats. Meaningful dialogue about use is now more a part of technology planning than it was in its infant stage in schools; however, dialogue always adds an additional burden of time and collaboration to the system.

Science Versus Art

The mere mention of "machine" sends the artistic community into a tailspin. Images of teaching becoming so much of a science that it takes away from the art of teaching is a long-standing concern. Technology pushes this concern further by suggesting that an information system will require bringing the artistry of teaching to the level of discrete data. The concern that "bits" will never describe the whole is quite real. Therefore, at many meetings, people are dealing with their fear of science as a singular way of describing teaching and learning.

Once again, this sparks the political debates within a system. Rather than understanding the balance between quantifiable information and qualitative information, people see them as either-or.

The challenge for us is to understand what in qualitative information can be quantified (as we have begun to learn powerfully with the use of scoring rubrics) and what in teaching and learning defies describing explicitly. The greater the possibility of turning our information into knowledge, the greater is the possibility that we will we be releasing our creativity as artists.

Long-Range Building and Short-Term Demands

Technology has insinuated itself into our lives in ways we hardly notice. We used to be willing to use a computer that brought type to our screen one pixel at a time. Now, if the words don't appear instantly, we are impatient. We cannot wait more than a second or two for messages to appear on the Internet. We are accustomed to instant return on input.

Schools cannot operate with that sort of immediate turnaround time. In order to be thoughtful, school personnel need to have time to process the information they receive. Analysis, synthesis, and decisions about resource allocation require study. It is surprising, given the mission of schools, that there is little time for them to be learning places. This will change when we learn how to use the feedback spiral for our learning and get a better sense of the time it will take to complete a cycle for a given problem or set of data. This is the "strategic" aspect of providing education—applying the learning that has emerged from within the organization and from the larger environment. To think strategically about improving education means to be able to step away from the "brush fires" to see the bigger picture.

Conclusion

The challenges are great; the possibilities are limitless. We have come to live the experience of how the Chinese people define *crisis*. The Chinese character means "opportunity" and "crisis." It suggests that we are in a time of both opportunity and crisis.

The crisis we are facing is the crisis to public education as we struggle to maintain a system designed to educate our democratic nation. In conjunction with the advent of technology, we are observing a larger number of home-schooling students, a greater inclusion of special needs students, more research and information about teaching and learning around which to process and shape practices, and a potential voucher system based on accountability information systems.

The opportunity is that we are finally able to do what we believe all educators have wanted to do for many years—create a science for teaching that does not ignore the art of teaching. We can finally bring all of the incredibly rich and artistic experiences teachers have developed to the fore, and so bring the wisdom of teaching to the larger education community. We can analyze data about student learning in ways that were previously too laborious for classroom teachers. We can communicate with one another and connect to one another in ways that were either costly of our time and finances or impossible. We have joined an international community of educators all able to build knowledge around the complex acts of teaching and learning.

To meet the challenges posed by technology with the aim of improving student performance, we will need to follow a path of continuous growth and learning.

References

Costa, A., Kallick, B. *Discovering and Exploring Habits of Mind*. Alexandria, Va.: Association for Supervision and Curriculum Development, 2000.

Jacobs, H. H. *Mapping the Big Picture*. Alexandria, Va.: Association for Supervision and Curriculum Development, 1997.

Index